Hi, my name is PINKY

A singer's lifetime in the limelight

Pinky Steede

Hi, my name is PINKY

A singer's lifetime in the limelight

Pinky Steede

MEREO
Cirencester

Mereo Books
1A The Wool Market Dyer Street Cirencester Gloucestershire GL7 2PR
An imprint of Memoirs Publishing www.mereobooks.com

Hi, my name is Pinky: 978-1-86151-421-9

First published in Great Britain in 2015
by Mereo Books, an imprint of Memoirs Publishing

Copyright ©2016

Pinky Steede has asserted her right under the Copyright Designs and Patents Act 1988 to be identified as the author of this work.

A CIP catalogue record for this book is available from the British Library.

This book is sold subject to the condition that it shall not by way of trade or otherwise be lent, resold, hired out or otherwise circulated without the publisher's prior consent in any form of binding or cover, other than that in which it is published and without a similar condition, including this condition being imposed on the subsequent purchaser.

The address for Memoirs Publishing Group Limited can be found at
www.memoirspublishing.com

The Memoirs Publishing Group Ltd Reg. No. 7834348

The Memoirs Publishing Group supports both The Forest Stewardship Council® (FSC®) and the PEFC® leading international forest-certification organisations. Our books carrying both the FSC label and the PEFC® and are printed on FSC®-certified paper. FSC® is the only forest-certification scheme supported by the leading environmental organisations including Greenpeace. Our paper procurement policy can be found at www.memoirspublishing.com/environment

Typeset in 11/16pt Century Schoolbook
by Wiltshire Associates Publisher Services Ltd. Printed and bound in Great Britain by Printondemand-Worldwide, Peterborough PE2 6XD

Preface

This book is dedicated to Michael H.W. Wall, my husband of 35 years. Thank you Michael, for allowing me to be someone's wife, someone's mother, and most of all, for allowing me to just be myself. It's been lovely.

Also to my mother and father, and all six of my brothers and sisters – especially my late elder brother, Webster, without whom there are many things I would not have got to do off the Island – and only because he thought I was the best. But then, they all did. I will be forever grateful.

Michael, I love you!
Pinky
(November) 2015

Contents

About the author

Chapter 1	'This is the first day of the rest of my life'	P.1
Chapter 2	Growing up in an island paradise	P.9
Chapter 3	Teenage love	P.17
Chapter 4	The Holiday Island Revue, 1969	P.24
Chapter 5	The Gene and Pinky Steede Show	P.31
Chapter 6	Bubbling Brown Sugar, 1978	P.37
Chapter 7	Hong Kong	P.53
Chapter 8	Return to Bermuda, 1994/95	P.80
Chapter 9	Discovering Portugal, 1995	P.87
Chapter 10	A hurricane and a charity show, 2004	P.99

About the Author

★★★★★

Pinky Steede is an international singer, dancer and actress who was born in the British Islands of Bermuda on September 15th, 1941. After a career in Bermuda, Britain and Hong Kong, she settled in Portugal and has sung in most of the large casinos in the Algarve and most of the major hotels as well.

She performed at a very early age all over the island of Bermuda until she left for Britain in 1976 to make her home off the island.

In 2000 she was invited to do her first Bermuda Jazz Festival, since which she has done two more in the sublime company of such great performers as Aretha Franklin, Patty La Belle, Seal and Joss Stone, with whom she shared the bill.

In 2008 she was invited to Strasbourg by the Bermuda Government to perform for the Bermuda Board of Tourism. In 2009 she was inducted into the Bermuda Music Hall of Fame.

She lives with her husband Mike in the village of Paderne in Albufeira, Portugal.

CHAPTER 1

'This is the first day of the rest of my life'

I cannot tell you the number of times, indeed the number of years, when I have started the year, the New Year, with that phrase, because it never ceases to focus me on whatever new project I am about to undertake. Since I was a small child I have always thought, very seriously, that I have a story in me. In fact, I am very positive there is. So here goes!

I don't remember my grandparents very well. My grandfather, Alfred Charles Joynes, who was a tailor by trade, passed away before I was born.

I know more about my grandmother, Eliza Joynes (nee Outerbridge), my mother's mother. She was a startlingly beautiful, very elegant woman, a thespian who performed with the Unity Dramatics and the 20th Century Dramatics, and was considered Bermuda's leading actress of the 20th century. I will quote from Mrs Nellie E. Musson's wonderful book *Mind the Onion Seed:*

Her acting went beyond the Theatre. Eliza Joynes had her own 'Glee Club', she directed numerous musical productions, and gained great popularity for her banquets and funfairs at the Alexandrina Hall, where her banquets were generally held. Young men in fine evening attire, which included frock-tail coats and gold cufflinks, would step lightly from horse-drawn landaus and escort laughing young women dressed in wide-hooped gowns with lace and frills and flowers in their hair, to the gala banquet hall. Waiters in morning dress would stand to attention while waiting for Eliza Joynes, the actress, to go to the honoured place at the head of the long banquet table.

Wow! Thanks for that, Mrs Musson. Now I know where I got my entertainer genes from!

My mother inherited her talent from her father, because she was a wonderful seamstress/tailor.

I am so sorry I know so little of my grandparents. This I can put down to the fact that they disinherited my mother when she chose to marry my father rather than the man they had chosen for her.

My father was born in Bermuda on 13th October 1886 in the parish and island of St David's, and as everyone on the island of Bermuda knows, the inhabitants of St David's are racially mixed. In fact, for quite a long while they looked like white people, and I am absolutely certain that old-time Bermudians will remember not really knowing what the mix was. Remember?

When my father was born his surname was Pitcher, and I believe I am related to all the Pitchers, Lambs and Foxes on St David's. I knew my father as James Tyrell Caisey all my life, because when he left St David's he apparently took his godmother's surname as his own. And so, my family name, from then on, has been Caisey, but we know where we came from.

My father crossed over the bridge into St George and lived there for a while, working on the ships which ran in and out of Bermuda on a weekly basis to New York. In fact, I remember many years later my older brothers doing exactly the same thing on the *Queen of Bermuda* and the *Ocean Monarch*. The ships my father worked on for a while were called 'Lady Ships' or 'Lady Boats'. My father rose to be a qualified chef on these ships, until he had an accident which cut off the tops of his fingers on one hand, which really put paid to working in that occupation. He was unable to cope with the loss and, of course, not being able to work, he turned to drink. Consequently, by the time I was aware of it, I don't remember my father as anything other than liking a drink.

I really did love my dad. He stayed at home, unable to work because of the accident to his hand, while my mum worked in the linen department at the Hamilton Princess Hotel. Dad took me to school each morning, but he had a battle to get me there. I would wake up in the morning, always with some plan to get out of going to school. I remember my dad carrying me to school under his arm, with me saying 'Oh Dad, I don't feel good today'. He had an American twang in his voice – possibly through working on liners – and I always remember him saying 'Frances, are you telling me lies?' He always called me Frances, never Pinky. We had the funniest times together and I just wanted to be with him while all the rest of us were at school. We got to be very close.

Because my father had been the head of the house and the breadwinner, and was unable to fulfil these roles after his accident, my mother had to go out to work. Keep in mind, of course, that she had been raised to 'make pretty', play the piano and sing around it. But her forte was the tailoring her father had taught her. She could sew, she made drapes, curtains, lace doyleys, wedding dresses – in fact, she made her own and her sisters' as well - and she sewed for other people too. But she could not cook; in fact she could not boil water when she and my father were married, and my father did the cooking. So when he had the accident, she took her tailoring trade in hand and went out to work. She secured a job in the Linens

Department at the Hamilton Princess Hotel. In fact she was in charge of all the linens - sheets, tablecloths, making absolutely sure that these things were all in good order. Let us remember that Bermuda at the time catered to extremely wealthy people, in many cases members of the aristocracy, and in some cases royalty. Bearing in mind that all these hotels were only catering to white people at this time, we only got to work there, not to be part of it - *yet*. My mother worked at the Hamilton Princess for a considerable time. She also belonged to many of the Lodges and was a member of the Cathedral choir for many, many years.

All of this, of course, meant that I was taken care of by my older sisters, so much so that I remember thinking my older brothers and sisters could be my mother and father, perhaps because I did not feel as close to my mother as I should have.

My brothers and sisters were all singers, dancers, and/or musicians. My older brother, Webster Caisey, or 'Red' as everyone called him, was a jazz enthusiast, and had a great collection of long-playing albums (LPs) - so large, in fact, that he donated it to a new black music radio station on the island, ZFB. These albums consisted of the greats in jazz and pop music of that time. Webb was also a quite good dancer, being absolutely amazing in tap, ballroom and anything else he put his mind or feet to.

My eldest sister, Gloria, was the strong one, the matriarch, simply because she was the strength and backbone of the family. No one dared to step out of line with Giah - my name for her since I was a child. I'm sure it started out as 'Goya' for 'Gloria', but I much prefer Giah. Since Gloria could dance as well, she and Webb formed a dancing duo. They performed together in many of the local venues such as Alexandrina Hall.

Ruth, the middle sister, was the sensible one, the only one who has been married just once - to the same person for 63 years, while the rest of us all had to do it many times before we got it right! Ruth is the most wonderful person. My brothers and sisters are all lovely people, but Ruth is quite special - so kind, generous and thoughtful, just as my mother used to be. I fill up when I think of her - maybe that's because nowadays we live 2,500 miles apart.

On the Island the family are all addressed as Tilly Caisey, a family nickname, after my father. So when I got my cat 18 years ago (a ginger female) we decided to call her Tilly Caisey, so that I would not miss my brothers and sisters so much. But I digress - I'm sure no one is interested in my cat!

My brother Howard was the one who was so serious about life and getting ahead, and making a place for himself and his family. With all of that, while still a working musician/ singer and a fine performer, he still managed to build his own home with the help of his elder son, Anthony, and a few good friends, even though he was working seven nights a week and most times seven days with the day job - all the hours God gave him.

My two youngest brothers, Bill (Gilbert) and Albert (Whitey) Caisey, were the 'raves' of the day, and loved by everyone, especially the ladies. They were both musicians and singers, both played bass and both worked all over the Island in all the hotels and nightclubs, and quite successfully as well.

I suppose my upbringing was quite innocent, as Bermuda is not a sophisticated country. For example, in Bermuda there was no such thing as transvestitism, in contrast to a great many other countries. There were certain things which Bermuda was just not ready for, and it remains so even today. The Island was worried about too much of the 'new' ideas, and if I had not gone out into the wide world I also would not have been exposed to it.

It may seem surprising now, but my mother never saw me perform - it was not the sort of thing she did, even though I was singing at the best hotels. We have to remember that my parents were born way back at the turn of the 19th century, into a different age. As for me, I learned to see things differently. I could walk on the same side of the road as white people, even back then.

One of the reasons I am writing this book is that I hope Bermuda will realise, at some point, that there are quite a number of dreamers - young people like I was - on the Island, who aspire to do what I did - and to some degree they do, quite successfully. But it would have been so much more so if I had had the backing, and most importantly someone else's belief, in what I could have accomplished.

CHAPTER 2

Growing up in an island paradise

I have been truly fortunate to grow up in such a beautiful island as Bermuda. For those who don't live there, let me tell you something about its history and background.

The colonisation of Bermuda began in 1609, after Sir George Somers landed a flotilla on the island in a storm - it's said that an account of that storm was the inspiration for Shakespeare when he wrote *The Tempest*. But the island had actually been discovered more than a century earlier, in 1503, by a Spanish sailor called Juan de Bermudez. This was barely ten years after Columbus had accidentally discovered the

New World. Soon many Spanish and Portuguese sailors were embarking on 'joy rides' around the island, looking for treasure. Of course, Bermudez gave the island its name. The island is surrounded by dangerous reefs, which made it a dangerous place for those early sailors, and the seabed is littered with the wrecks of the many ships that have gone down there over the centuries.

Sir George Somers' ship, the *Sea Venture*, was one of a fleet of relief vessels that were taking much-needed supplies to the colony of Jamestown, Virginia. Fortunately, thanks to the hand of God, all 150 of those on board the *Sea Venture* survived, and the ship was rebuilt using timber from the cedar trees which were then plentiful on the island. The tales of this Atlantic paradise travelled back to England and the British came to the conclusion that this could be valuable territory. The first colonists began arriving in 1612, and set about constructing houses with thatched roofs. The first Anglican church was built at the same time, St Peter's in the parish of St George, and although it was hit by hurricanes it was rebuilt, again using cedar wood, and still stands today. The strong religious beliefs of the colonists have influenced the island ever since - they don't call this the 'bible belt of the Caribbean' for nothing. The church is said to be the oldest Anglican church in continuous use outside Britain. This means Bermuda's Parliament is the second oldest of all overseas Commonwealth countries.

According to a note by Ann Gordon-Smith in her 2015 Bermuda calendar, in 1620 the church was the location of the first General Assembly, when our religion, constitution and common law took root.

All our visitors know that we are protected by the warmth of the Gulf Stream, which is why our winters are so warm, with average temperatures in the 60s Fahrenheit - no frost has ever been recorded on Bermuda.

After my mother and father married they moved to Happy Valley Road, Smiths Hill, so called because the hill and the houses were owned by a Mr. Smith. We lived in a big old rambling house up on the hill above the Unity Patio and Tennis Court. In the very big courtyard of this large house there were two cottages. In one lived the Davis family, and in the other, my brother Howard and his wife and two children, Anthony and Keith.

In the big house lived my mother and father, with me and my youngest brother, and middle sister, Ruth, she and her husband Calvin having their own one-bedroom flat with kitchen included. My brother Bill and his first wife had the same kind of facility, and this was where I was born. My younger brother Albert and I had our own bedrooms, along with my mother and father. It was really a quite large house but it still managed, despite its size, not to have an inside toilet! This monstrosity was set across the yard - in fact there were two toilets, one for the Davises and one for my family. I hit the panic button every time I had to go in there as there always seemed to be the biggest reddish-brown cockroaches hanging on the inside of the door (no lights, just holes where shafts of light showed you your way). These cockroaches were big, with what seemed like four-inch wingspans, and to add insult to injury, they were flyers. To this day I am petrified of cockroaches.

As it was a big house, we of course had a piano in the parlour. This piano played a big part in the family's musical growth - Ah! But more about the piano later.

Growing up in a place like Bermuda was, as you can imagine, the most amazing experience, because at that time we thought it was the centre of the world. We were so young and innocent, we had the whole of Happy Valley, Smith's Hill, Curving Avenue and beyond - all that open area to play in, and tall trees to climb. We all attended Mrs Seaton's School, a private school with perhaps 50 kids. Charley, Willie and Junie were my best friends - Junie was really 'Junior' but that was too long a word for us to spend time saying it, so we didn't. Children of all ages, races, creeds and colours being able to run free - well, actually not *all* of us *everywhere*; we couldn't go everywhere we wanted because the Island of Bermuda was still so racially segregated. But because the place was beautiful and it had very little crime, no problems really - it was just the best place to grow up in. So if I am honest, we really did not notice the whole other side of life, namely the segregation. We knew where we could go and where we belonged but we couldn't go just anywhere we wanted, such as certain places like upstairs in the movies, the beaches on the south shore of the Island, or front entrances of all the hotels, but it didn't really matter to us because what you don't know really doesn't bother you. We were happy just growing up in such a beautiful country, surrounded by the Atlantic Ocean.

Thinking of the ocean reminds me of an incident which happened to us when we were very young, and I sometimes wonder whether it affected any of the other children in the way it still affects me. We were all at Devonshire Bay hanging out, swimming, playing in the ocean and being otherwise unruly, jumping off rocks, all kinds of stuff, showing off generally, when one of the kids jumped off and struck the bottom. Unfortunately he died. Ever since then I have been absolutely terrified of the ocean. Despite this, when I was about 45 years old and living in Hong Kong I took scuba diving lessons and qualified in Thailand, but to this day I am still absolutely terrified of the ocean, and consequently have never worked on cruise ships, despite many offers.

We, the gang, used to go down to the back of our houses on the Happy Valley Road side, climb the oleander trees and swoop down on unsuspecting people, frightening the life out of them. So we guys, along with Alfie, my nephew, Shirley and Louis Thomas and Sue May, had the Hill and surrounding area on wheels - we had the best time. At the time I bet we didn't think it, but when I've looked back, so many times, it was the best growing-up time ever. Why, with our roller skates we messed up the Unity Patio, which was also a tennis court and doubled at night for all the big dances, with the big bands of the time, such as Al Davis and Pot Gilbert. So many.

However, in my private thoughts I knew that I wanted to be a star. I didn't know what sort of star, but I knew I was going to be a star of something. Actually, by the time I was two years old I was driving everyone in the family mad, mad, mad, singing and dancing wildly about the house. The singing, I would imagine, was not so good, as I was only two years old, but the noise was big and strong - so big and strong in fact that it took me many years to handle it!

Along with the singing loudly and dancing wildly, there was also a lot of staring into mirrors and making faces, because I thought I could possibly be an actor. My brothers and sisters all allowed me to express myself - possibly overmuch! At this point I was still going to Mrs Seaton's School, which I had attended from the age of seven.

Until this time I was just this wild-looking refugee kind of person, climbing trees with Junie, Charley and Stanley Davis. There were only three other girls and they all had brothers who were older too, so we kind of hung around together. Other friends were Geanette Robinson, Shirley Thomas and our white girlfriend, whose name was Margaret Johnson. Margaret's family were really nice people - I remember her brother Morris was at the fire station for quite some time, and they had a brother whose name was Carl and a sister named Doris.

While all the girls were turning into finished little ladies - well, as close as you could get to in Happy Valley Road in Pembroke - I was a proper tomboy because I, of course, was hanging out with the boys, learning how to swear, fight and all the other good stuff. I remember my brother Bill had this really lah-di-dah girlfriend, swinging her hips and all that nonsense, trying to take my brother away from me. So we all climbed up the oleanders, after, of course, gathering some good-sized stones to pelt her with. Boy, did I get beaten for that!

All of this was around the same time as sitting my 11-plus to go to secondary school, but I had to switch from Mrs Seaton's to Central School for my last year, and at Central I got beaten up every day by the kids. They pulled my plaits, stuck my hair in the inkwells, called me 'cat eyes' and 'white cod fish' - I was so glad that was over when it was over and I could get on with going to Berkeley Institute. I guess today this is what they call bullying. It was just as horrible then as it is now. Bullying, racism, it all hurts the same and it affects your life in just the same, horrific way.

Because my brothers and sisters were all singing, dancing and playing instruments and everything else, we just happened to have the aforementioned piano in our 'parlour', and everybody used to come to our house for my mother's cantatas, so we'd all sing and play the piano. I should say here and now that I have never been able to play the piano. All my brothers and sisters could play by ear, but I couldn't even do that.

So we have now got to the time when the piano becomes important, once again - I told you it would - remember?

You could call me an overachiever, interested in most subjects I focused on - reading, writing, arithmetic, cooking and home economics, up to and including sports. I loved very physical activity, something which has continued - I don't want to just 'glow', I want to sweat too - and the way I see it, long may it continue.

When I was 11 years old my father died, quite suddenly. It brought a dramatic change in my life. My mother and father would never have agreed to my singing in nightclubs, even the major establishments on the islands. But the death of my father, triggered, perhaps, because of grief, set me on the path I would follow for the next 45 years. By this time everything was moving along towards what I wanted to do with my life and career.

But life sometimes throws curves at you.

CHAPTER 3

Teenage love

I am a major fan of the writings of Mrs Nellie Musson, especially her epic *Mind the Onion Seed*. I have this book sitting proudly in a special position on my bookshelf, for all to see. (This will not be a long chapter, but it is the launch pad for the rest of my story).

In Chapter 7 of *Mind the Onion Seed*, Mrs Musson speaks at length about *'Bermudian black women in the Arts, pre 1900'*, and she quotes the words of a minstrel song at that time. It goes like this:

Mama, keep the gates locked now
Mama, keep the gates locked

Mama, keep the gates locked
Mama, keep the gates
locked... too late.

You may wonder what this had to do with the Five Wonders - this will unfold.

My family had a wonderful family friend, Reuben McCoy. One night I was told by my family that Reuben and four of his friends were coming to our house to rehearse their new vocal group, called the Five Wonders. I remember going to school that day and being so excited, just waiting to see them rehearse.

They came to our house because we had the piano in the parlour. I remember so clearly, there was Reuben, Harold Landy, Stanley Davis and Neville Paynter; actually, the fifth new member did not turn up for the rehearsal. Reuben said they were going to be a close harmony group. They said they already had a few dates so they had better rehearse, using the family piano. I asked if I could sit in, Reuben said yes, and they were very happy with what I could bring to the group. Thanks to the family piano, that evening I became the fifth member of The Five Wonders. That night it was impossible to sleep. I was going to be a Star. It was all I could talk about when I went to school next day.

Mrs Olive Trott was our booking agent, and she got us work all over the Island, including the Mount Area Restaurant, the Clay House Inn and, of course, the

Angels' Grotto. We managed to create a really nice circuit for ourselves.

I was still in Berkeley Institute, doing quite well getting into my third year, but not being the overachieving student I had been, because to be a good student and a professional singer at the same time took a more sensible person than I obviously was - and a much more grown-up one. I wanted to do and be like everybody else in show business, so I dropped out of school. The only reason I was able to act in this way was because of my father's passing; this was a very bad time for me, because I could not fathom out why he had left me - I was not ready for him to die, and I loved him so much. This was when singing became so much more important for me, and stayed that way.

When Reuben McCoy was given permission to have me singing with The Five Wonders it was done with the instruction - the very strict instruction - that he would look out for me. Well, that did not keep the dogs from sniffing around, especially a certain Gene Steede. There was quite some competition building very slowly on the Island; my brother Bill had a vocal group, my brother Albert had a rock band, and then there was Gene, who was in a vocal group as well. As a boy of 13 or 14, Gene looked like Cassius Clay, the boxer, so he was good looking - and so said every other female on the Island. So I was in a competition, not only professionally, but personally.

But guess what, I was the winner. I always say

that I went from my parents' bed to Gene's, because at the time there would still be occasions when I slept with my mother when the mood hit me.

When I hit fifteen and a half, I discovered I was pregnant. Neither Gene nor I knew very much about the logistics of sex, the bottom line being that you only need one good shot at that age and the deed is done; in fact, six weeks after we had initiated the act, I was pregnant. Thank God my father was dead, because otherwise I most certainly would have been. Then I had to tell my mother, who was just not prepared for this kind of thing from me - there was I, thinking that you surely had to do more than that, and at least more than once. But in hindsight it was probably a good thing that it happened that way, otherwise I would not have been married or had children until well into my thirties, because I have always been so intent on what I wanted to do with my life, which was always meant to turn into my career.

The Five Wonders was a great learning experience, but I was beginning to feel I wanted to do more. I need not have worried, because a change was coming. That change came in the form of Don and Elsbeth Gibson, a retired acting couple from America, who were used to performing in theatre and on television. They were the best thing that happened to six Bermudian performers, all black, who became known as 'Don Gibson's Holiday Island Revue'.

I married Braxton Eugene Steede Sr., better known as Gene Steede, on April 28 1958. He was probably the most gifted musician and entertainer of his generation in Bermuda, and we performed together as Gene and Pinky Steede. Together we had a son and a daughter. We were married for 17 years. We had a great time, but the best part of our marriage was of course our children. Our son, Braxton Eugene Steede Jr. ('Jay'), and our daughter, Crystal Bianca Simons Steede, were both born on the Island and they both still live there with their partners and children.

Having my son and daughter was of course the best part of the first period of my adult life. I can still remember the joy I felt when my beautiful son Jay was born on 25 October 1958. But I had a hurdle to get over before I got my big moment. My mother would not allow me to nurse (breastfeed) for any longer than six weeks with either my son or daughter. Quite honestly, I didn't feel there was anything unusual about this because that's what my mother's generation just did - it was where they came from. Her generation had always nursed, so it was fine with me, and the six weeks was fine with me too - after that you slimmed down to what you'd normally been. Six weeks was long enough to be pudgy, having been pudgy for the nine months previously, including through the heat of the Bermudian summer! No problem there, whereas today, new mothers agonise over so many anxieties - 'How is it going to affect my child if I don't nurse? Is it something I should worry about?' And other guilt-ridden questions like those, but quite frankly with my generation it never crossed our minds. My mother had eight children and nursed every one of them, so the six weeks for each was plenty enough for anyone to cope with. We were confident mothers with happy children.

Jay and Crystal were both walking by the time they were ten or eleven months old. Because they were housebroken, I could take them anywhere and in some cases put them in quite adult company. They were very clever little people. The wonderful thing about this was that it was a mixed bag of races, creeds, colours, which I thought was marvellous for both children, and found amazingly stimulating.

The one thing I learned from marrying so early, so young, was that all four of us were deprived, emotionally and physically and intellectually. Our horizons sometimes - no, most times - were limited, while our ambitions made us too materialistic.

To help the finances in the early years of our marriage it was suggested that maybe I could take up what could be called a 'day job'. Most Bermudians had two or even three jobs to make ends meet, and I realised I would have to do the same thing. So I found myself employed at The Woman's Shop, which was a department store - as big a store as you can get on a little island like ours. It was owned by the Gibbons family, a member of which became our Prime Minister.

My career there lasted for about ten minutes. Imagine it - up all night performing, taking the children to school next morning, rehearsing, and working at the store! I just could not be this kind of working wife and do the whole thing, so I had to inform the top lady that, much as I would like to fulfil my obligations, I just could not do it all - my career was what I had to do in my life - and I am glad to say that she was OK about it.

I was married to Gene for 17 years, but the truth is, we both pretty much knew it was over after only four years. Things began to go wrong, and we both started to see other people. We divorced in 1971. At the end of the day, I finally divorced my husband because I did not want to be in a relationship where both of us were seeing other people and were still married to each other - I was not one of those women who could do that, and even more importantly, I do not condone this kind of treatment of people, and never did or would. It has to be remembered that pretty much everywhere on the planet is bigger than Bermuda - it's no more than 15 miles as the crow flies from end to end. It's such a small country that if you walk out of your front door and sneeze, everyone knows you have a cold.

So why did I wait so long to split up? I wanted to wait until my children had a chance of understanding. Did they? Do they? I shall never know for sure.

CHAPTER 4

The Holiday Island Revue, 1969

I have always considered Don and Elsbeth Gibson the lifesavers of the six young people who ended up in their show, the original Don Gibson's Holiday Island Revue. I was not a part of the first auditions, because I was at home pretending to be grown up with my now second baby, a girl this time - at 17 years old. When these auditions took place, if I remember correctly, they had chosen everyone, including Gene Steede and my brother Bill, as well as a large group of about 16 people, such as Bryan Butterfield, King Trott and Dennis Smith, to name but a few.

The show would consist of a man and woman duo,

a quartet, all male, a couple of lead singers, a man and a woman, and a dance group. When they chose the guy and girl duo it was discovered that the girl had young children, so her mother would not allow her to perform because the show would be working six to seven nights per week at six or seven of the major hotels - Great God Almighty! - such as the Hamilton Princess, Elbow Beach, Castle Harbour, Sonesta Beach, Harmony Hall hotel, Bermudiana and Belmont Manor.

At this time we were finally being allowed to work in the principal hotels in the major rooms, the 'night clubs'. But of course we ourselves weren't allowed even to pass through the grand front entrances of these glittering pleasure palaces. Why - simply because we weren't white. We could only get in through the service entrances. Imagine that today. However, we were discovering that even this was beginning to be a step in the right direction. At least we were getting over these thresholds, and with all the optimism of youth we could feel that things were a-changing. So we allowed the big 'suits' to treat us in the way they wanted, without kicking up Holy Hell about it. Nothing was going to stay the same, that much we knew, and we knew too that the 'suits' would have to change with the times. I remember the Gibsons playing a major part in kicking over the traces in those optimistic, progressive days.

So we, the young, eager performers on the Island, went and stood in line to protest at the cinemas, the beaches, just anywhere, and we would walk around Hamilton with banners, proudly, orderly, politely, because we had been brought up to be polite - no arrogance, no bad behaviour; true bad behaviour to mankind on the Island was part of its past, all tied into the cultural beliefs and dark, unspoken suspicions which were now becoming distant history, best forgotten.

We fixed ourselves so effectively into these changing days that soon we were allowed to sit anywhere we wished in the cinemas - previously we hadn't even been allowed to sit upstairs, which was the reserve of the white colonial British, the Americans, the non-blacks. We'd had to sit in allocated black areas downstairs - mixing of the colours even there was a no-no. We'd never know how it felt to go into the major restaurants or onto the beaches, but all that now had to change, and change it most certainly did.

You know, I believe God has watched over me all of my life - all through my career. A major disappointment for a young girl singer in that duo with my then brother-in-law, Calvin Steede, was turned into a major blessing for me because my brother Bill, my sister-in-law Junie Caisey and Gene all suggested *me* to the Gibsons. So I got to audition - thank you, Jesus! Because I had always had the dream, and I had always known what I wanted.

Professionally speaking, this was the best thing that had happened to us all; firstly, we were the first all-black show to go into the hotels, thanks to the

Gibsons. We were also able to actually work in a job that we *wanted* to be doing. Don't get me wrong, Bermudians to this day still have two and sometimes three jobs just to break even, because the cost of living in Bermuda has never been anything less than very expensive.

For those readers who have never seen Bermuda, do go and see it. It is the most beautiful island. I might, or must, add that we changed a few things too; for instance, we, 'The Revue', refused to go in by the back entrances of the hotels any more because we thought that if the tourists who were coming to see us in such great numbers really appreciated us as much as they seemed to, then we were worth that little bit more respect. In fact, I remember being a major part of kicking over the traces in a great many instances at home, in Bermuda.

When I begin my show I always start my saying 'My name is Pinky and I was born on the most beautiful island in the world, and I know this because I have worked on most of them.'

The Revue ran the show that first season with such an amazing amount of success that it was decided we would be kept on, but not with the same number of people, so from 16 or 17 of us it was cut down to six. Now it was Junie Caisey, Gene Steede, Bill Caisey, Dudley Brown, Gene Ming and Pinky Steede. We were on our way to showing what we could do individually, and together as a group. And oh my, we were good!

Our Musical Director, Jim Gregory, chose the six of us for our individual singing talents. Dudley Brown was a basso profundo, Gene Ming was a tenor, as were Bill and Gene, and I had, still have, the loudest voice in the world. I was born to work in theatre because my voice is loud and very clear and I don't necessarily need a microphone except, of course, to preserve my voice. Junie Casey, who was married to my brother, was a soprano with a light, clear voice.

I'll never forget the night the six of us were performing at the then Castle Harbour Hotel for a very large group of Americans from the southern states, and when we got to the closing number, the rousing *Battle Hymn of the Republic*, they all to a person got up and walked out. Well, we didn't know quite what to think - it must have been American politics! And just a little different from the evening at the Sonesta Beach on the South Shore, when the astronaut John Glenn walked into the room in the middle of the show and stopped it dead in its tracks. Nothing could follow a John Glenn!

I remember singing the day President Kennedy was assassinated. Never was I so ashamed of another human being as I was of Lee Harvey Oswald. It was the hardest thing, but we had to perform to a very high standard that night.

We continued to work with the six performers for a few years, but then of course as the show got better we got better too, going from strength to strength with our dancing, acting and singing. Finally the Gibsons got the idea that we should have two shows, completely different, running side by side with the same six-performer cast. It was tough, but we just couldn't get enough of it. It was hilarious, and the pattern went something like this. The band would open the show, while many beautiful people would be elegantly drifting in, taking drinks or sitting down to eat if it was a supper club evening, and we would come onto the stage. Our performance lasted for one whole hour, interwoven between the six of us; we all danced, we all sang and acted, making maybe six, eight, ten costume changes, beautiful, beautiful colours, all of us always immaculately turned out. Even though we had a dresser backstage we all helped each other to dress perfectly - remember, these were the days of lime green, shocking pink, South American-style à la Carmen Miranda. Sometimes we sang phonetically in Spanish because, of course, Bermuda was initially a Spanish island, discovered by one Juan de Bermudez.

So we, as youngsters, were 'winging it' - enthusiasm wins over experience. We put our hearts and souls into just everything we did, and we were doing well. Until, one day, along came a professional dancer from New York's Broadway, at the invitation of the Gibsons, a Ms Sally Neil, who did all of five to seven minutes with the Revue each evening, while we still did our full hour on stage, moving shaking and singing. Ms. Neil was a brilliant, gorgeous girl, built like an athlete, black of course, so you're no doubt getting the picture, and my, was she good.

But please remember what I said previously, that all our attitudes were developing along with our professional abilities, and the biggest of these attitudes was, of course, our egos. The trouble was, Sally was so very good that we felt our egos being severely hit. And oh, the size of her pay cheque - per minute - and oh, the anger! But it taught us to stand up for ourselves and we said to the Gibsons, politely, for we were taught never, never to swear, 'Tell us what more you want us to do and we'll do it, and pay us more - we want to be recognised for what we are'. After all, we had mortgages to pay, cars to run - yes, we did have cars - and kids to feed and clothe. We were at last feeling that we had made the grade and were ready to be treated financially better. We were growing, and, as I say, confidence was growing, expectations were growing.

So, what happened at the end of the season? Surprise, surprise, Sally disappeared. She'd no doubt got the message and of course we were over the moon, not with any feeling of acrimony but simply because we'd faced the situation and had dealt with it. We were growing up in one of the toughest of businesses.

CHAPTER 5

The Gene and Pinky Steede Show

By now of course, as well as getting quite well-known on the Island, we were doing well in North America, the West Indies and other islands. The Gibsons were wanting to expand the Revue and wanted to take Gene and me out for different performances. Gene and I were absolutely knocked out when they invited us to go to New York to perform on the Hugh Downs Show out of New York City. Hugh Downs was the Jay Leno of the early morning shows.

So off we went to the Big City. And I do mean big. I mean, when you were born on a 23-square-mile island everything is big. New York has always been my favourite city in the world - the energy and excitement of this place is like nowhere else. That's only my opinion, of course.

We had an appearance on the 10.00 or 10.30 am show, which we did, but before that we had to do the publicity for the Bermuda Board of Tourism - of course, in our very own Bermuda shorts, and for Gene a Bermuda 'skort' (a cross between a skirt and shorts) and, as the pictures show, it was funny. We are actually pictured there, in beautiful summer island clothes, shorts, skort and wonderful plaid Bermuda shorts made by Trimminghams of Bermuda, for many years a household name on the island, on the skating rink at the Rockefeller Centre. They did try to put us on skates, but I'm sorry to say our ankles were just not strong enough. It was hilarious because we couldn't even stand in them!

However, we weren't entirely happy with someone taking control or advantage of our performing and earning powers, as we were feeling ready to go and spread our wings on our own together. All this past experience really had made it very obvious to Gene and me that we should develop our own show - 'The Gene and Pinky Steede Show' - which is exactly what we did, and a winner it certainly was.

So we left the Holiday Island Revue after 10 years, and went on our merry way, doing all the same hotels and nightclubs as the Revue had done, but now it was just the two of us. That part of our lives and our working lives was just as successful. We went on to become household names, and it was quite wonderful.

Gene and I had the wonderful opportunity to go to Canada to perform in Ottawa, at the Château Laurier Hotel, on a two-week gig. The hotel was gorgeous, and, as its name suggests, it had known a palatial former existence. It was packed full of people, with lovely big rooms. We had the most wonderful orchestra, and at the end of the night I would end with 'Somewhere Over The Rainbow', because my big voice reminded the bandleader of Judy Garland - it always brought the house down, and I ended up every night of the gig sitting in with the band after that. It was a good gig.

We just loved Ottawa, so beautiful. The snow was as high as me, and I had never seen snow in my life. But the cold - oh my, that cold!

At the end of the two weeks we went with a lot of the hotel guests to the Banff Springs Hotel ski resort in the Rocky Mountains, where we were to do a couple of nightclub shows. I didn't know much about mountains. The morning after we arrived we scampered like kids from our cabin and went out into this wonderful winter wonderland, and just ran and ran across the snow to see where we'd be performing. Suddenly I felt I was almost having a heart attack, due to the thin air, I guess, but I soon recovered from both the pain and the embarrassment.

Later I somehow got into an aerial sightseeing flight looking down on this scenery to die for, when I had the quite wonderful experience of learning to fly a plane in the Rockies. There we were, just the pilot and me. The plane had a steering wheel that lifted out and could be moved over to the second passenger. So, while I was enjoying being in amongst the mountains for the first time in my life - in fact I was absolutely knocked out with it - he asked me 'Would you like to fly?' This, of course, was after I had told him that I had always wanted to learn to fly, but that it would cost too much money. He passed the wheel to me - literally passed it to me - and said 'It's just like driving a car. If you want to go right, turn right, and if you want to go to the left, then turn left. Just lift it up, down, whatever you want.'

So I did. It was the most fun, spoiled only by the fact that he wouldn't let me land the plane! In an instant I knew I'd got myself a new career as a pilot if the singing ever folded up.

In exactly the same way as the Revue had developed, we developed too. But by the time Gene and I had been married for 16 or 17 years we knew the writing was already on the wall, and in the same way as the members of the Revue had grown up and away from each other, both musically, professionally and personally, so had Gene and I. So in 1971, after 17 years of marriage, we were divorced. Gene left the Island, to the chagrin of all the lovely ladies who had been only too happy to watch him perform.

I picked up all our previous contracts and was soon

back on the circuit of all the major hotels. But it wasn't very easy for me to do this, because I was given custody of our son and daughter, and to have to keep them as the only breadwinner, with a mortgage, electricity, telephone, school clothes and food to pay for, seemed so much more serious now that I was on my own.

However, from this shattering situation came the Pinky Steede Show. I had got ready for this and kept all the same nights - six or seven - pretty much as I wanted and needed. It was of course a hard slog and very frightening, and still I did not make enough money. I remember very vividly my older brothers and sisters bringing me food to help feed us all, so it was not a pleasant time, or, for that matter, easy. But as my mother used to say, 'God only gives you as much as you can handle'. I got through it and had five or six quite successful years as a solo artiste on the Island.

Then - here we go again. One night I had just finished performing at the Sonesta Beach Hotel, the pearl of all the Island hotels, spectacularly perched high on a cliff on the south shore and its golden beaches. Then, would you believe it, as I was walking back to my dressing room, this guy, who had described himself as an American producer, came backstage and introduced himself as Danny Holgate from New York. We got into conversation, and after we had been chatting for a while, he said, 'I have a show running on Broadway called Bubbling Brown Sugar with a cast of all-black performers, and I want to ask you a question.'

'Yes' I said, 'What is it?'

He replied (rather naively, I later thought), 'Have you ever thought of working on Broadway?'

Well - is the Pope Catholic? I picked myself up off the floor - I had been laughing so hard that I had fallen over. So we just stood there and chatted some more. He was a big producer, and not only did he have 'Bubbling Brown Sugar' running at one theatre on Broadway, he had 'Guys and Dolls' running at a theatre in London - again, with an all-black cast. When I asked what I would be doing, he said 'I know you're actually black, but are you always that tanned?'

I'm naturally fair-skinned and blue-eyed, so I explained that the tan was paler in wintertime! I asked him what he would do if I came to America. He explained that he could not promise me anything because the producer and director, a man called Eubie Blake, would have to see me. He knew I could sing, but the choreographers would have to look at me. Well, I knew I was done, because I was only a singer who moved well and never in a million years was I a trained dancer, so I was sure I was dead in the water.

Anyway I flew to New York and met everybody and sang for them. But I guess everyone has a shortcoming, because... they accepted me!

CHAPTER 6

Bubbling Brown Sugar, 1978

And so began my great odyssey, and the future was indeed looking to be a very promising one. Danny told me I would have to audition, and there were no assurances that I would get the part, but he couldn't see why I shouldn't. So that's what I did. I flew to New York City and auditioned, in a cold audition room somewhere off Broadway.

Imagine my horror when I was introduced to the whole of the management team of BBS! They asked me if I was ready and I said 'yes, please', and just did the song, which was Shirley Bassey's 'Never Never Never', an amazing song which suited my voice as well as it did Shirley's and Barbra Streisand's.

I'd had to go and take dance and tap classes as I wasn't very good at either of these, but I was by now a polished performer and could sell myself really well, so by the time I opened my mouth for them, because I was used to working six or seven nights a week 50 weeks a year, they knew I could very easily sustain a full show, even on Broadway.

Before I left the audition I was told I would be hired. I imagine the feeling I had could only be matched by winning a 50 million dollar lottery prize.

Danny said he would be in touch, and I went back to Bermuda to work, but the word filtered through that they didn't have all the financial backing in place to mount a show like BBS on the West End. A musical, like any show, needs lots and lots of money up front. It was almost a year before the show was set to go, so while all this was happening Danny put me in 'Guys and Dolls' on Broadway as an understudy to several parts for six months while I waited to be called to London.

All the auditions in New York and England having been run, I then had to wait for all the rest of the cast to be chosen, all the sets, the singers, dancers, actors, costumes, orchestra. This show was going to land on the West End of London, the motherland for me, because I was a British subject, from the British Island of Bermuda. 'Bubbling Brown Sugar' was the first black show to go to the West End for 52 years. It had perhaps three or four white performers and all the rest of us were black, and might I add that this was possibly the first time for many of us that being black had worked in our favour. I was just so, so proud. The show featured music by Fats Waller, Cab Calloway, Count Basie, Duke Ellington and Eubie Blake. In fact the original music was composed by Emme Kempe, a protégé of Blake's.

Years later I met Eubie Blake in New York - by then he was 90.

On arriving in London, having been engaged to perform in BBS, I was to receive stage coaching, but of course the producers needed to know that I could do eight shows per week and still be able to sustain my voice. I said I had never had lessons, but I had worked 52 weeks a year. So they arranged for me to go to Ian Adam, a really nice man and a mega-talented, respected voice specialist in Kensington, who was absolutely wonderful. He told me 'I am not going to give you lessons, because what you have is a very natural gift. You breathe properly, you hold yourself properly, which is all very natural, and we don't want to make that any different, so just come and do vocal ease'. By this he meant scales, for instance, which I did.

Yet I found the show very hard. Rehearsals went on every day for 10-12 hours, for six weeks. Not only did I have my own part to rehearse, I was covering three other vocal roles as well. Despite this I was always keen to be with Ian early in the day, part of the long list of top performers who were under his wing -

Sarah Brightman, and the adorable Michael Crawford, for instance. Michael was this slim, softly-spoken, gentle guy from BBC TV's 'Some Mothers Do 'Ave 'Em', who emerged into the world success of 'Barnum' and 'Phantom of the Opera', which began in the West End in 1986. He was just a lovely guy - didn't say a lot, worked very hard, and being with him showed me just how down-to-earth British performers are. Here he was, already a big TV star with 'Some Mothers' and now I could see him growing in stature and voice while he was getting ready for Phantom and Hairspray, and now he was preparing for another West End role. A really nice guy.

That wonderful singer Elaine Page was getting ready to go into Jesus Christ Superstar, and at this time she was looking for children who would be suitable to perform in it with her, so she was frequently backstage at 'Bubbling Brown Sugar', because its cast featured many children, both black and white, as would 'Jesus Christ Superstar'. She was still waiting to hear whether she had got the lead role. She was already famous, having starred in the musicals 'Cats' and 'Chess'.

I also met the Welsh-born singer Shirley Bassey at this time. Shirley was absolutely stunning and very, very focused. She used to come backstage at BBS. She and Elaine Del Mar were friends, and it was Elaine who took me under her wing. She knew people I knew in Bermuda, so when I got into BBS Elaine guided me.

Although it was going to run at the Royalty Theatre in the Strand, all the rehearsals took place at the world-famous Theatre Royal in Drury Lane, Covent Garden. You don't need me to tell you about this particular world famous-theatre, but I will anyway! The Theatre Royal is the most beautiful of theatres, and probably the most famous. It has ghosts, they say, but even if that's true it is a fabulous place, and for me this was not just my first time in the West End but my first theatre job. I was so honoured just being there. How crazy was that, coming from a little island in the middle of the Atlantic Ocean? What are the chances of this sort of thing ever happening to a person? Very, very slim, I can tell you. But nevertheless, it did, and I was proud to represent my country.

And of course, I was part of the most beautiful cast on the West End of London (five miles). The music was all from the 'Big Band' era, featuring music by Duke Ellington, Billy Eckstine, Cab Calloway and Billie Holiday, to name but a few - everybody who was anybody at the time in the twenties and thirties.

On the night of the first performance of BBS I remember, just before the curtain went up, standing on the stage in a circle with the cast, saying a prayer and realising I was standing in a puddle of my own tears - I was so pleased that I had managed to get there. From a very early age my ambition had been to get to Broadway or the West End of London. Because I was a British subject this was the easiest option - England, the Motherland.

All the kids in BBS went to eat between shows on Friday or Saturday afternoons or evenings. To our great delight, one night, sitting in one of the booths, was the actor James Earl Jones - 'The Voice', specifically the voice of Darth Vader in 'Star Wars' and Mufasa in 'The Lion King', among many others. Of course we went right over and started to annoy him by asking him just to talk, so we got the whole experience of his voice (and of course his autograph). When he laughed his whole body shook. What an experience, and what a pleasure!

At that point, although I see it clearly now, it had never actually occurred to me that I had amassed all the necessary experience and stage technique, both British and American, while growing up in show business on Bermuda, to equip me with all the essentials for London's West End. Who could possibly have thought that a kid from such a tiny island would find herself in the centre of where it all happened? It was truly amazing, and I think about it a lot, even now. The Gibsons, with all their TV experience, had always said to me 'See that back wall of the theatre? That's where your voice has to hit'. On those early Bermudian stages, with sound equipment which could suddenly blow up so that you were well and truly on your own, I learned where my big voice came from. It was truly astounding, and the richest training any performer could be fortunate enough to have. So there I was, fortunate indeed, on this incredible stage.

The show was a tremendous smash hit, thanks primarily to Billy Daniels and the very beautiful Elaine Delmar - she was so beautiful to look at, it was shocking. She was African dark, while I was more fair skinned. We won the Evening Standard Award for the Best Show of 1978, and also the most beautiful.

First of all, Elaine was a stunningly, blindingly beautiful woman, black, tiny short Afro hair, great African singer - not only beautiful, but a beautiful person in every way. She was in so many genres of entertainment including Shakespeare, a great actress and singer who knew how to move well, although Elaine probably wouldn't have called herself a dancer even though we all danced together on stage. She was the lead female star in 'Bubbling Brown Sugar', with Billy Daniels as the male lead.

The choreographer was Charles Auguns, a six foot five American who could dance his butt off and thought everyone should be as good as he was - and rightly too. Billy Daniels was at this time a truly major singing star in America, starring on Broadway as well as the West End. Although classed as black, he was in fact quite fair-skinned, with straight hair and blue eyes. One day I asked him if he was going to wear make-up for the stage, to which he wryly replied: 'Well, they'll no doubt put some stage make-up on me but l'll never do a black and white minstrels look - I know who I am and if those guys at the front of the show don't think I look like a black singer, then, well, tough.' He was a lovely man. As so often happens when you've been as big a star as Billy for so many years, you can afford to be nice - it's natural to you.

Of course, none of these accolades were earned easily. Each show was two and a half hours long, and on Friday and Saturday there were two shows, each two and a half hours, back to back. We were also contracted to rehearse every day and do promotional work when required.

My proudest moment came when I was commanded to appear at the Berkeley Hotel, Berkeley Square, for HRH Prince Charles, in a charity show which featured the music of Sammy Cahn. It was a fantastic evening, and after the show we were introduced to Prince Charles. And, ladies, he was really quite good looking! In the weeks before the show we were interviewed by security people who we supposed were responsible for the security of the Prince. This must go on all the time. I remember reviewing my life to date, hoping I had never done anything which would affect my being in the show, but everything must have been OK.

I was surprised to find that we were not being put up in the same hotels as the white guys. But for me, a kid from the Island, this is what BBS showed. It really just laid the whole black and white racism situation out in front of me. So it was an extreme learning curve for me in my life and in my work. I have never worked in the southern states of the US because I could never stand to be looked at the way the people down there looked at a black person.

The requirements of the BBS contract were very strict and we were expected to comply one hundred per cent. Even so, I loved it - absolutely loved it! But, my God, it was hard work. We did and two-and-a-half-hour shows every day, and two shows on Fridays and Saturdays back-to-back. And then there were all the rehearsals and all the promotional work we were involved in. We cast members were very fit, but not in such great health. We were coming down with illnesses one after another, and it seemed to me I had a permanent cold. The doctor had to come most days to give us Vitamin B shots. I was not at all used to the English weather - I still cannot bear it! I am indeed an 'Island child'.

Of course, we all came down with one virus after another. The management of the show were quite sympathetic and gave me a week off to go home and rest, so I did. I went home to rest in Bermuda, had a lovely week in the sun, got myself a tan and went back to London. Then, of course, I discovered that the contract demanded that you do not go past a twelve-mile limit from the theatre, so after all that I was fired!

I promised myself that this would be the last very big mistake I would make in my life - and so far, so good. The way it should have panned out, you would have thought that as I was a British subject and my country was a British Colony, I should have been protected in some way by my country, and my mother country, but that was not the case - then. Now, of course, you can move from one country to another and work wherever you like, for as long as you like.

As you could imagine, I was not at all happy with this - no, much worse than that, I was devastated. But in some strange way I completely understood where the management was coming from. It would be impossible to mount a West End show without very strict rules and regulations to protect the investors.

But I was not completely alone. I had met a man, a wonderful man, one night. He came to the show with his brother-in-law and at the interval he sent a message backstage via the doorman. Nothing gets past the doorman which doesn't belong there! God must have been looking after us that night, because the doorman passed the message on to me. The message asked, very politely, if I would have dinner with him after the show, and if so, he would meet me in the theatre bar. Actually - and ladies will appreciate this - our eyes met during the first half of the show, and there was chemistry between us already. I spoke to the girls in the show and we all ran to the hole in the curtain to have a look at this man - they all gave me the thumbs up!

His name was Michael Wall, and he had come to the show with his brother-in-law, John Wood (now sadly passed away), after Mike had made arrangements with the stage door manager to meet me in the theatre bar. John was married to Judy, Mike's only sister, who is now one of my dearest friends. John quickly instructed me that he had told Mike to say nothing, as he would do all the talking. He said it would be better that way, as Mike could be quite boring!

And this is how those two clowns spent the evening. I had one of the best evenings of my life. Mike and I both realised there was chemistry between us. In fact it was the first time in my life I had ever actually been courted. Michael and I have now been together, married, for 35 years, and thankfully we still have that chemistry.

After my dismissal from BBS I began to realise that I wasn't really the big 'I am' I had thought I was. I remember conversations with Billy Daniels, a lovely man, who kept asking me what I intended to do after BBS - would I carry on and try to work in England, or would I go back to Bermuda? I didn't know how to answer his questions, as I was being pulled in both directions. Despite advice from many people, I had not thought about getting an agent to look after my future bookings, and the slow realisation was beginning to seep into my brain that I had not been looking after my business.

My very good friend Elaine Delmar came to my rescue when I finished BBS. Other cast members had their contracts extended and so did Elaine, but she had two contracts which she could not pick up, so she passed them to me. They were two three-month tours - one to Portugal, the other to South Africa.

Before these tours I had been invited to perform at the Bermuda Festival. I asked Mike to come to Bermuda to meet my children and my family. Like me, he had been divorced for a few years, and he had two great young boys. We decided we would get married in Bermuda, and we did it, very simply, at the Bermuda Registry Office. My brother Bill and his girlfriend of the time stood as witnesses, and afterwards we had a wonderful lunch with Mr and Mrs John White. John was an old friend of mine and if I remember correctly, he was one of the organisers of the Bermuda Festival, but please forgive me if I am mistaken.

My family organised a reunion at Shelley Bay for the family to meet Mike. I recall him asking how many people would come. I replied that I really did not have much idea, but I said it could be a hundred or so, as we had a really big family. We had a good laugh after the reunion, which by the way was lovely, because Mike said it seemed to him there were more like 2,000 guests! He was bowled over. He had never seen so many skin colours, and thus began his black race education. It did not faze him, and he has been in love with Bermuda and its people ever since.

We could only stay so long on the Island once we had made ourselves legal by getting married, because Mike was General Manager of a construction company on the south coast of England and I had still contracted to do some shows.

Before closing the BBS chapter I should mention the good things, professionally, which came from the show. I was given the chance to appear in a very popular BBC show in the UK called 'New Faces'. It was quite a simple format - you just did your performance in front of a panel of showbiz judges, and if you were very good, you won; if you were not so good, you didn't. It was in reality a variety show with scores. It became a very successful and long-running show in the UK and discovered quite a few people who became big stars, including Marti Caine, Lenny Henry, Victoria Wood, Les Dennis, Patti Boulaye, Jim Davidson and the band Showaddywaddy.

In my first show, I won, so I had to return for the final a few weeks later. Amongst the judges was the female impersonator Danny La Rue, who was to remain a friend until he passed away in 2009, and the TV presenter Michael Aspel. After you did your performance they each in turn told you what they thought. In reality it was all a bit of a blur, but I do remember Michael Aspel telling me that I was going to be quite a good cabaret artiste.

Imagine my horror when I was beaten into second place! Ego is a terrible thing. The winners were Bucks Fizz, a two boys, two girls band who went on to become very famous and successful. They'll always be remembered not only by their catchy number in the

Eurovision 'Save Your Kisses For Me', but the way the girls whipped off their skirts at the end of the singing to reveal tiny minis! All in good fun.

I was naturally disappointed not to have won the second round, and will always remember Michael Aspel taking me to one side and saying in that beautiful voice of his, 'Well, you might not have won this time, but you are going to be an amazing cabaret artiste'. He had a meltingly gentle way and knew how to handle someone like me at that low point, I'll never forget that. He was another lovely man whom people adored.

The BBC also invited me to go to Ireland - Dublin, actually - to appear on the Jackie Trent and Tony Hatch Show. Jackie was a great British singer and Tony, her husband, was a very successful composer, songwriter and producer. I did not know at the time that these people were major superstars in the UK. I loved it! I realised that I could now treat rehearsals in a very much more professional manner. All thanks to BBS.

Jackie wrote material for just everybody, all the big stars, and what a writer she was. So l and most of the 'Bubbling Brown Sugar' performers went to them to do the show for Eire TV and it was lovely, just marvellous.

While I was there in Ireland I went to meet all the Caseys (my Dad's name) - all related to me in some way. The musicians we'd been rehearsing with told me, 'Go into any pub, just say you're a Casey and you bet they'll all stand up, hug and celebrate you'. Wow, did it work!

I seemed to do OK with the BBC. I have no idea why - maybe there is a BBC-type person which fits. On BBC radio late at night there was a very popular music programme called 'Through 'til Midnight'. I was told that by law, the BBC had to broadcast a certain percentage of its music output live, i.e. not just playing records, so I would get the train up from Portsmouth to London in the morning, with my music, meet the BBC Orchestra - what an orchestra! They were the pick of Britain's top musicians. We would record the show in the afternoon and it would be broadcast at 10 pm that night.

In the UK there was a very famous band called the Ted Heath Orchestra, and when Ted Heath passed away, so did the band. A few years later it was reformed under Stan Reynolds, who was the lead trumpeter in the original band. It recruited Dennis Lotis, who was the band singer with the original band, and I was recruited as the female singer. I did not really get to know Dennis, as we only met for rehearsals and shows. Singing with a high-class band was like going to heaven, and we did Sunday evening concerts with never an empty seat, supported mostly by the older generation who had grown up with the bands. When we went to Hong Kong I reluctantly had to give up this gig, and it was with tears in my eyes, I can tell you.

Denis had a great voice and used to sing with Lita Rosa. I never worked with Lita because she was already performing with the Ted Heath Orchestra. For someone like me, young and starting out in the big time for the first time, watching Denis was like taking a masterclass - that is how well this guy sang and performed on stage. If he was anything to go by, Lita had to be his equal, and I know now just what a celebrated couple they were. Dennis one day asked me to tell him what I thought was the difference between working with a big band like the Ted Heath Orchestra and working with one of the others, and I said I thought the difference could be summed up in one word, maybe two - professionalism and dedication.

Remembering now, I recall how I was always very, very tired after performances, because working with those big names made you give your absolute all. Between auditions and the actual performing I could easily lose five pounds in weight without trying - the stress was there, but when you're giving your best that's just the way it is. Not having learned to read music I had to work extra hard to learn my arrangements very, very thoroughly, so that when I hit my mark I didn't embarrass myself or any of the musicians - it just was not an option. Of course, when I'd been younger I thought I knew all this, but experience now with the big boys taught me to learn very quickly and very well.

My actress grandmother, Ms Eliza Joynes

My mother and father on their wedding day

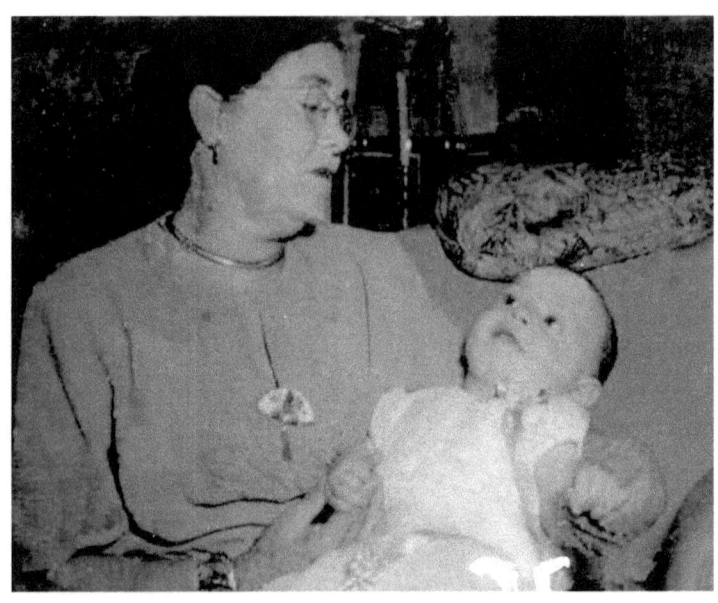

My mother babysitting

Tomboy Pinky

Me with my brothers and sisters

Smile please – Gene Steede, my boyfriend, my brother Bill Caisey, Reuben McCoy of the 5 Wonders and my brother Albert Caisey

Holiday Island Revue

Holiday Island Revue

With my brother Bill, Holiday Island Revue

with Gene and Dudley Browne

With Gene

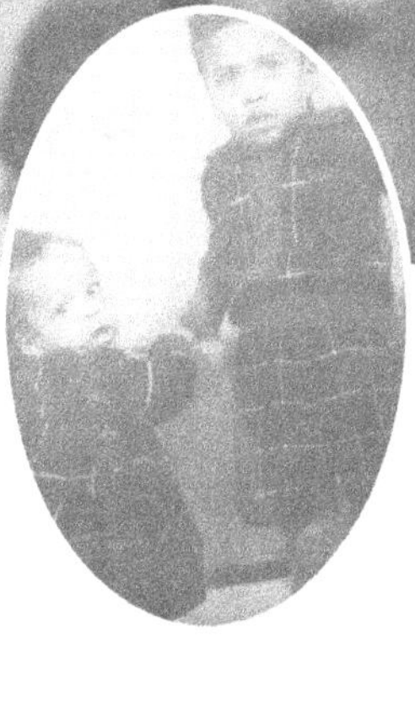

Our children Jay and Crystal

Publicity photo for Bubbling Brown Sugar

Poster for Bubbling Brown Sugar

My marriage to Mike at
Bermuda registry officer

Gene with our
granddaughter Jamie

Mike's boys Justin and Matthew

The Several Poses of Pinky Steede

Although a number of Bermudians have become international performers, including Frank Crichlow, better known as Frank Johnson, a singer and composer during the thirties, and present day performers, none have been better known than has "Pinky" Steede. From the time Mary Frances Steede, "Pinky", began singing in the fifties with The Five Wonders, to her Command Performance for Prince Charles in 1978, her love and enthusiasm which she has displayed in her work has not lessened.

Originally, co-performer with her ex-husband Gene Steede, she performed throughout Bermuda, and across Canada and the United States. The star

"Pinky" Steede—An International Entertainer Mary Frances-Steede

In 'Mind the Onion Seed'

At the Pink Giraffe with the Little Big Band

In rehearsal for Guys and Dolls, Hong Kong

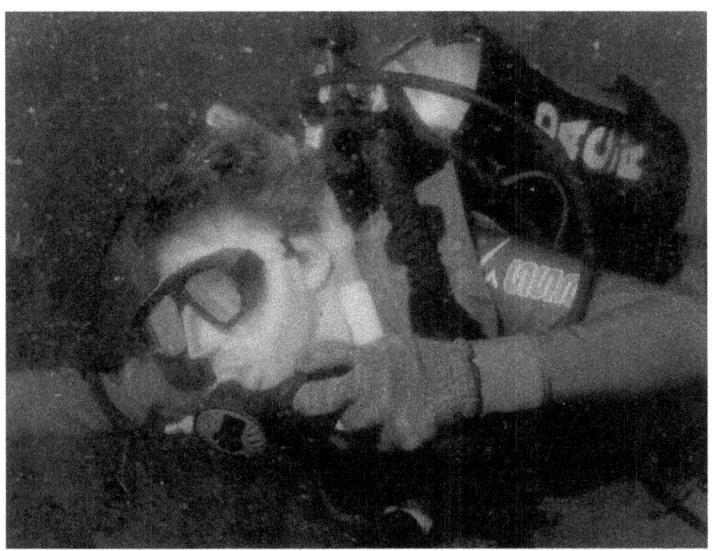

A qualified PADI diver

Mike and me, Hong Kong

BERMUDA Philharmonic SOCIETY

ALVIN FERREIRA MEMORIAL CONCERT

MOZART REQUIEM

Soloists:
BARBARA HOWSON - Soprano   NANCY CHISLING - Contralto
BRIAN SEMOS - Tenor   PETER NASH - Bass

**BERMUDA PHILHARMONIC CHOIR
BERMUDA PHILHARMONIC ORCHESTRA**
Leader - *Suzanne Dunkerley

EPILOGUE - TWO FERREIRA SONGS
arranged by GRAHAM GARTON

'The Day John Lennon Died'
Soloist - PINKY STEEDE

'Shades of Green'
(Chorus and Orchestra)

Conductor - **GRAHAM GARTON**

THE ANGLICAN CATHEDRAL
Sunday 6th November 1994 8.00 p.m.

Tickets $18.00 ($12.00 for Seniors and Students)
Available from The Harbour Master, Opus 1, Meyer Travel and Philharmonic Members

* By courtesy of the Menuhin Foundation

I was so proud to sing with the Philharmonic in Bermuda

Mike built me our first house on top of the rock.

Publicity poster, Bermuda

Another night at Henry VIII, Bermuda

Casino publicity photo

Publicity photo, Portugal

Café La Rose poster

Show poster for Evita Forever

Publicity poster, China

That's me at the back – with my clothes on!

Papa Mike with my granddaughter Morgan

Papa Mike with my grandson Warren

Our first house in Portugal

In Evita Forever

Evita Forever, night club scene

The cast of Evita Forever

With Mike's sister Judy

'Dishing the dirt' with Sandy Butterfield

A visit from Crystal

A technical meeting with Pat and Syd Purvey at the Southampton Fairmont Hotel for the PALS concert

CHAPTER 7

Hong Kong

After Mike and I were married we returned to the UK as a newly-wed couple, and loved it. The hard part came a few days later when he took me to the airport at Heathrow and said goodbye, so that I could start my three-month tour of South Africa. It was not easy for either of us, but we both knew it had to be done for the sake of my future in show business. Thankfully, we were older by now, and more mature, so we were able to cope as a newly-married couple being apart for three months.

I cannot express how truly excited I was about going to Africa - for me this was truly the motherland, of course, no matter what nationality you were, black, white or indifferent. It was during apartheid when I went to South Africa that all the i's had to be dotted and all the t's crossed before boarding the plane, because with apartheid at the time and the political problems, you did not want to play around. I was told the one thing you must never play around with was politics - ever. I was told that immediately I spoke, I would have no problems, my accent being very mid-Atlantic. The people, all the musicians, black and white, were excellent. All I had to do was present my music and we were away.

The tour of South Africa was for the Holiday Inn hotels, and took me to my 'second motherland'. It took place during apartheid, and to go there was a little scary, especially for me, being black with a very fair skin. I was told to make sure that all my paperwork was in order, because my Union - Equity - would not help me if I got into any sort of problem there, and for God's sake, not to get involved in any part of politics. However, I was also told by a really nice guy at the Union not to worry, because as soon as I opened my mouth they'd know I was not 'African'. He also said they had a test there that they used in order to discover if you were black. This was done by the police and Immigration. Was that true? I have no idea!

My three-month tour of South Africa in 1980 took in the countries of Lesotho, Botswana, Swaziland, Zululand and Gabon. When you had the time, you did as many tours of the country as you could. This was Africa, after all - the wild animals, lions, tigers, elephants; the palaces - well, the palaces for the kings or chiefs and the straw huts for the many wives. And they each had a number of them!

When Paul Simon recorded and published his famous DVD 'Graceland' I ran out to buy it, not just for Paul Simon's songs and performances, but to experience, once again, African musicians - unbelievable! I would arrive at the hotel, give the bandleader my music, and the following morning when we rehearsed they would be note-perfect, and so lovely with it. Therefore, the shows were wonderful and very well-supported.

Most of the country was wild and totally spectacular - lions, tigers, elephants, the lot. The earth was a very bright terracotta, and I was really in awe of the springboks, the agility and beauty of them, and I bought and carried a pair of carved springboks back to England - they travelled for years as part of our belongings and they still have pride of place in our home.

That tour, as I said, was for three months, and took in Gabaron, Masaru and Lesotho, Babotswana, Botswana and Swaziland. One of the many daughters of the King of Swaziland was the hostess of a night club there, and she saw to it that we had tickets to get into the club, which was lovely!

When I arrived back in England Mike was at the

airport to meet me. He was a senior executive with a construction supply company on the south coast of England, and at the time we were living in Portsmouth, on the south coast of England. During the journey back to the house he told me that he had been asked to transfer to the Hong Kong branch of his company. He wanted to go, but was concerned about how it would affect my career. Mike was a totally committed sort of guy, with a very good work ethic, and was always dedicated to his company. Anyway, during the journey home we decided we would sleep on it and continue the discussion the following day.

It did not quite work out like that, because within the hour we had decided that Hong Kong was to be our next great challenge. I had reasoned that with me it was 'Have Voice, Will Travel', and the whole idea of living and working in Hong Kong and, of course, South East Asia, greatly excited me, so we would be very stupid not to go.

When we decided to leave England and go to Hong Kong to live and work we did so because it was the best thing to do at the time, financially, physically and mentally in every way possible. And, so said, so done. It was God sitting on our shoulders, directing us, making sure that we did what we had to do, the best possible thing for us, our lives and our marriage. Every turn we took, every person we met, every job that was given to me, every new hotel that opened its doors to me, every new group of musicians I met and had the marvellous opportunity to work with and learn something from. It was the best - places, people, things, always the best place for us to be, the best work we were going to do until the next thing came along.

A few weeks later Mike was gone, leaving me behind in England, because I had a few weeks' contracts to fulfil. I really hope everyone gets the chance to go to Hong Kong, because it is very difficult to describe it in words. The way I felt about coming from beautiful but sleepy Bermuda into a metropolis which was at work 24 hours a day was really beyond my vocabulary. The one thing it did have in common with Bermuda was that it was another British colony, with all the good and bad that that brings.

Bermuda has a natural beauty formed by God and its people, and Hong Kong has a beauty that comes from the beauty and diversity of its architecture, combined of course with the ability of its people to enjoy the rewards of sheer hard work. Factories work 24 hours, seven days, with people from all over the world working side by side in complete harmony. Hong Kong takes each day as it comes, and deals very successfully with the many problems which each day produces.

I found that because the Hong Kong people were short and dark-haired, I looked rather like them. If we were in a group you would not have known that I wasn't a Chinese - I was their height - so, wanting to keep my individuality, I changed all that and went blonde. After that I knew I'd pulled it off because the Chinese - especially the guys, who in those days were pretty tactile - would turn to look me full in the face, not able to place where I was from, something of a rarity. I thought this was very interesting, so l bought right into it, because it worked for me on stage and off.

Mike was busy with his job, settling in, and then I arrived from England, so besides his job he also had a jet-lagged wife to introduce to Hong Kong. He had a nasty habit of working late and I soon found myself having dinner on my own and thinking that I had to do something about it. When it comes to dealing with problems, it's wonderful getting older as you find you are better able to deal with them. Mike dealt with this first problem by giving me the job of moving us out of the Excelsior Hotel, where we had been living, and finding a house for us to live in.

I can't think of a better way to get to know Hong Kong. Within about two weeks I had found a small gated estate out in the New Territories in a new town called Shatin. I loved it - there were European and Chinese living there. Mike was in shock because he thought we would actually be living in Hong Kong but he didn't complain, so we moved into Shatin.

Some years later we moved to Yau Yat Chuen. Anyone who was anyone just had to live in that area - a picturesque, marvellous, affluent area where, not unusually, luxury came as standard. Jackie Chan, the Hong Kong martial arts movie star, lived close by, and for Michael, after a day on building sites surrounded by giant trucks, bricks, sand and cement, Yau Yat Chuen was the perfect chill-out zone to come back to, as it had become for all the expats who were doing well there at that time. They had everything they could possibly ask for, or that money could buy. But, and there's always an eyebrow-raiser in any perfect situation, Hong Kong's airport, But Kai Tak, was so close that you could count the rivets on the planes as they flew overhead. This, combined with a nerve-racking right turn when they were close to the ground, made it something of a spectator sport, but one we weren't sorry to lose when the airport was relocated. We didn't miss the jet fuel perfume in the air one little bit.

We soon settled and got to know the neighbours. Luckily one of them, Robert King, who was Chinese despite the name, was big in the fashion business, so of course he knew a lot of people, and he pointed me in the direction where I was able to meet the right people to get my career going again, namely big swanky hotels like the Sheraton, Holiday Inn and Hyatt. And so I started working on it.

I remember, when we first got to Hong Kong, going to one of the major hotels there to attend a meeting with a food and beverage manager. Having dressed in jeans and stiletto boots, I was sitting feeling very uncomfortable and being made to feel even more so because people were surreptitiously looking at me. It finally dawned on me. Well, let's just say I never went job-hunting dressed that way any more. But I did get the job!

The time came for me to leave Hong Kong to do a three-month tour of the Portuguese casinos - Casino do Alvor, Casino de Montegordo and Casino de Vilamoura. This was absolutely wonderful - big bands, and three to four speciality acts from all over the world. I had not had this sort of exposure since BBS, and I thorough enjoyed myself. The venues were always full, six nights a week. They fed us three times a day if that was what we wanted, but you never had time to put on weight because we worked every night and rehearsed long most days. I was born for this!

During my three months in Portugal I fell in love with the country. The people are dark-complexioned and of mixed race like me, and they are wonderfully generous of spirit. The weather is just like Bermuda except for three weeks in the winter when the chill winds come down to say 'hi' from Siberia, and in July and August when the temperature has been known to hit 47°C up in the hills. The beaches are nice, although not like Bermuda, and the sea is cold - again, not like Bermuda.

Any spare time I had I spent on the beach, always in conversation with someone. All the beaches had little restaurants on them, selling fish just caught the night before, so quite often I would have a plate of sardines - just wonderful! And potatoes and a salad - what on earth could be better than that?

Most of the people running the restaurants spoke better English than me and they were fascinated by the fact that a large proportion of Bermudians were Portuguese. I failed to meet a single Portuguese person who knew that. They loved it when I explained that my sister Gloria's husband, Willy Moniz, was Portuguese - that seemed to make me one of the family. It was from these early beginnings that my love affair with Portugal began.

When I arrived back in Hong Kong, organising our new house was my first objective. At the same time I was educating Mike on the wonders of Portugal, as he had already told me he had never visited the country. He then suggested that the next year we could spend our holidays there, on the Algarve. That, I realised much later, was a very clever way of calling off the Portugal conversation.

I was beginning to make some friends. One, Linda Chiu, a very nice Chinese American, became a close friend, and we used to go to Phillip Wain, a great health club, to work out and then hang out together. Linda was as American as apple pie and such a breath of fresh air. Her husband Henry, was a senior guy in the construction industry, just like my Michael, and they were good friends together. We all were. If Michael and Henry had to go, say, to Korea or Japan on business, they would take us with them so that Linda and I could have a holiday while they were working every hour God gave them -the construction industry in Hong Kong was in its infancy and those two guys were helping it grow by the day.

I remember going with Linda to Canton from Hong Kong for a one-day tour and ending up at the very large open-air market filled with many, many interesting items - clothing, food, shoes, linens, all beautifully embroidered tablecloths and napkins, silk jackets - so, so beautiful! Pottery, all with the China blue that China is so famous for; dinner sets, serving dishes with cover and platters. Needless to say, when we finally left Hong Kong it travelled back with us, and I can assure you that I still have most of it - I guess because that was where Mike and I spent our early married life.

Also at this market they sold food, everything you could think of - every kind of meat and vegetables. The meat consisted of cow, chicken, lamb and pigs, but you had to pretty much keep moving because it was very hot and humid. The smell could be quite overwhelming. I got to one carcass and was just standing in awe, staring at the animal, and trying to figure out what it could have been, and when it finally dawned on me, I felt the colour drain from my face because I was staring at a dog, completely stripped of its skin - skinned - and now all the stories came home to roost. I mean, we had eaten snake, which I thought was much like chicken. And we had heard about the monkey brain, where a monkey is given alcohol and put under a table with a hole in the centre of it, and then hit on the top of the head (the monkey, that is) - and everyone takes a spoon and dips in while the brain is still quite warm. True. I leave that to you to figure out. But cultural differences are vast and varied.

Linda and I were having lunch one day in the Sheraton Hotel in Kowloon when we were approached by this tall, good-looking man who asked us whether we had enjoyed our meal and if we were happy with the service. His name was Thomas Mueller and he was the Food and Beverage Manager. It had been a very good meal, and we told him so. We continued to talk and I told him that my big ambition was to work in the Pink Giraffe, the Sheraton Hotel's famous nightclub. He asked me where he could see me working in the next few weeks, and sure enough, he turned up at one of my shows. I did not see him leave, so I thought that was it.

A few weeks later Linda and I were in the Sheraton again, and who should walk by but Thomas Mueller. He said hello, asked how we were, and offered me two weeks in the Pink Giraffe - just like that! By now I had met some really good freelance musicians, all Filipinos. We formed the first of my 'Little Big Bands', and performed at the Sheraton for many months, in the Pink Giraffe.

I think I would have to say that was my favourite job in Hong Kong, with my first 'Little Big Band'. These guys were five of the best Filipino musicians I have ever worked with. They wrote music as well as reading it and played out of their skins. They also helped me to learn and sing a Chinese song called 'Shanghai Beach', from a famous Chinese soap opera. And of course they would fall over laughing when I made a mistake, which was often!

Six nights per week we worked in the Pink Giraffe and on Sunday we took a busman's holiday and went to Ned Kelly's Show Bar, where there was straw on the floor. And it was fabulous. We could try out stuff there before we quietened it down and took it back to the Pink Giraffe, which was an extremely elegant room. Ned Kelly's was not the highest-paying gig in Hong Kong but on a Sunday evening it attracted some of the best local and visiting musicians on the island.

It was well known that if you did well as an entertainer at the five-star Hong Kong Sheraton, you were on the road to sure-fire work at other prestigious engagements. Could this maybe happen to me?

Ned Kelly's was a raucous, popular music bar at the top of the street and truly a fun, fun place to work. We used to make as much noise as we wanted while we worked out our arrangements, with straw on the floor to deaden the sound, in preparation and rehearsal for our show the other six nights a week in the Pink Giraffe, the epitome of elegance on the top floor of the Sheraton, in Kowloon.

Anyway, every Sunday evening this guy would come into Ned Kelly's and without fail he would ask me to sing something of Ella Fitzgerald's, which I happily did. Afterwards we would chat, and always he would say to me, 'You sound just like a young Ella Fitzgerald', which amused me, but also flattered me, because just how many young Ellas were there around? There couldn't be many, so I regarded this as a sincere compliment. This went on for quite some time, but with no strings. Truly that's all there was between us, but somehow it was a nice link, a sort of mental compatibility between us. It just sometimes happens that way between the audience and a performer.

On the opposite side of raucous, The Pink Giraffe was just fabulous - a swank supper club, discreet, quiet and elegant, where opulence just oozed. It seemed to be on the circuit for visiting performers from all over - from America came The Platters, Sarah Vaughan, Elaine Delmar, the Scissor Sisters, and from Britain came Max Bygraves, and - remember these - The Inkspots! As well as our own numbers, the house band and I played them on and played them off - just marvellous.

Yet the showbiz side of life never really attracted me. I enjoyed the people, but I always remained in control of my life and did not become prey to anyone who was a controller, unlike some singers. I worked hard to get where I did, never exposed myself to overbearing people. Filipino performers are similarly minded - they are amazingly talented and hardworking, and superb musicians.

I had so much good luck with my work in Hong Kong considering the fact that no one knew me, but I think that in such a place word gets around very fast as to whether you're good or bad. One of my real problems was that the majority of the good entertainers were ethnic Chinese - this is a given, as well as the fact that over 90% of the population were Chinese. I am not complaining, as this is exactly as it should be of course.

I remember Mike and I and some friends were out to dinner one evening at the Holiday Inn in Kowloon when a gentleman stopped by the table and said 'Hello, Pinky Steede from Bermuda'. Well, you could have knocked me down with a feather! He told me he was the new President of the Hotel Hyatt, another big hotel in Kowloon. I really felt embarrassed as I knew his face but could not for the life of me put a name to it. He told me that he used to be the General Manager of the Inverurie Hotel in Bermuda, and Gene and I used to work for him there. He then said he had heard I was in town, and would I like to do New Year's Eve at the Hyatt? I nearly jumped down his throat. 'Yes, please!' I said.

It was the strangest night of my career. The clientele were nearly all Chinese, with a few Europeans. I opened my act, but it didn't get the reception I expected. The applause was muted. I can't say it was a show I really enjoyed, until the end, when the Chinese audience, to a person, stood up, and all brought me a single red rose. It was amazing! I loved it, and was extremely grateful. This turned out to be a very long association with the Hyatt, with them naming dessert dishes of all sorts after me - quite amazing!

Mike continued to be very successful in his job and was involved in some of the biggest contracts in Hong Kong, including the building of the Mass Transit Railway, which was the underground railway system. He was also involved in Hong Kong's amazing social housing programme, tower blocks rising a floor a week - it was unbelievable!

Before we knew it, we had been in Hong Kong for eight years, and although we enjoyed it very much I was beginning to miss my family, and wishing I was back in Bermuda. I started having conversations with Mike about how I was feeling. He was still too young to retire, and he knew he would not be able to work in Bermuda. The months went by and one day he said to me that if I wanted to go back home, it would be OK with him, so, after organising his replacement, we said our goodbyes to Hong Kong and went back to Bermuda.

It was lovely to spend time with my son and daughter, and with family and friends. I was lucky enough to get two shows each week at the Grotto Bay and Sonesta Beach Hotels, and we were quite satisfied with that.

But you know there is a saying, 'You can never go back'. First of all, people think you have changed, and I can understand that, but I don't really think that it is *you* who is different, but actually the other people, thinking you are. It seemed to create many problems you would never associate with just 'going home'. At any rate, within a year or eighteen months of returning, I very stupidly made the biggest mistake of my life by speaking of the work situation on the islands, locals as opposed to expatriates. Now it has been a long-held belief of mine that Bermudians should at least be considered for any job on offer. I will return to this subject in more detail in Chapter 8, Return to Bermuda.

We spent many hours working on the little house on the South Shore, and we so loved doing that, but as the months went by I realised that 'going home' really was not what I needed to do. Mike and I had discussed it, and he never complained. In those days there were no cellphones or emails, and I had not realised that he had kept in touch with Hong Kong. He said to me that he had to go back to Hong Kong regarding some unfinished business, and he would be back in a week. When he came back he told me he had been offered a General Manager's job with China Resources, which is the commercial arm of the Chinese Government. He would be tasked with starting a new ready-mixed concrete company for them, which would be called 'Red Land Concrete' for obvious reasons. I jumped at it, and within a few weeks we had picked up and returned, once again, to Hong Kong. Going a second time was much easier compared with our first time. I know my job was first, to find somewhere to live, and then to furnish it, and in doing this, remedy the mistakes we made the first time.

When we were back in Bermuda I very much enjoyed my two gigs per week, and it was beginning to dawn on me that even if I was not working six nights a week it was not really necessary. I was getting older and more mature, or at least I hope so!

My first job travelling outside Hong Kong for me was at the Dusit Thani Hotel in Thailand. The Dusit Thani is a Royal Hotel, and whenever the Royal Family of Thailand was going to Bangkok they always stay at the Dusit Thani. This was a quite prestigious hotel, and I performed there on quite a number of occasions. There was an invisible but very clear division between the theatrical area and the nightclub salon. Theatrical performers were not allowed into the nightclub salon, or to have any conversations or mix with the audience. This was all very different from Europe, where you can speak with anyone.

I would have to say that Thailand and Bali were possibly my two favourite countries in South-East Asia. The people are known for their wonderful manner and kindness, always smiling, and Thailand is known as the 'Land of the Smiling Sun'. Bali for me is exactly the same. I remember we were running there early one morning - I do exercise no matter where I am travelling, except now, I walk. But I call it 'have sneakers, will travel'.

One day we ran past a young woman selling or bartering things, and she had the most beautiful kaftans, tie-dyed as only the Thais can. But she did not want me to buy them, she wanted to barter them - for my running shoes. So what're you gonna do?

Try finding a proper pair of Nikes when you want them - no, need them - in Bali, where you could find any number of fakes but never the real thing. I also loved Phuket in Thailand, but no matter where you walked in Phuket, a wild seaside resort, you could smell the sewer, and this went on for years. But they had a couple of venues there, and one had a very, very old Thai lady playing piano and singing. She was absolutely wonderful! We saw her on every trip there for years.

The other one was the Green Bottle. This venue had a five-piece Thai band and they were good. I used to go there just to sit in - brilliant! Along with opening the brand-new waterside hotel the New World, with the Tony Cruz Big Band, and going to Taiwan with the John Meir Big Band, I think I had an amazing eighteen years, all told, in Hong Kong. The John Meir Big Band were a very popular band in Hong Kong. Taiwan society was very elevated at that time and the luxury knew no bounds. We also did gigs together at the Hong Kong Royal Yacht Club. Life was a ball, and a high-rolling one at that.

John Meir was an English teacher of music at one of the international Hong Kong schools. He was a singer and piano player who mainly used his out-of-school time as an arranger, and we worked together at all the notable venues - the Royal Hong Kong Yacht Club, the Royal Hong Kong Golf Club and the five-star hotels such as the Peninsula. These were big, serious gigs where you got to meet all the rich and famous of Hong Kong at its glittering best, so if you did well there, you had made it. There was such an ambience, such meeting and greeting between the politicians, industrialists and those who had no need to advertise themselves. I have to say that my performing clothes were just the most beautiful - they had to be, for luxury came as standard. The band leader and I were given equally regal treatment, with our own table and space to eat, drink and feel really special,

It was, looking back, just a different world in those colonial days, and l shall never forget our performances on a high balcony of the Peninsula, looking down on the audience, with an atmosphere of wonder and thrill pulsating through all of us. We always took care to respect our audience and play the music they particularly wanted, be it jazz, rhythm & blues or big band stuff, and it seemed to work so well. Like nowhere else on our performing journeys, these people actually tipped us, and generously too, which was an accepted thing only in Hong Kong; it was a place of such high energy, high achievement and high ego that if you delivered what they wanted, they made sure you knew it. And you always got asked back! Somehow this hardworking, self-motivated society felt right to me - a hardworking performer - and I felt we just recognised this in each other.

A new hotel opened in Kowloon called the Regent. It was magnificent! The rumour was that it would be designated a six-star hotel. It had a huge white marble staircase coming from the mezzanine floor into the main lobby - it took your breath away.

I was one of the acts invited to perform on the opening night. Me, 4 ft 11inches, standing alone on this grand staircase - unbelievable!

I was also given a lead role in the Hong Kong production of 'Guys and Dolls'. I played Sgt. Sarah Brown, of the Salvation Army. I was quite surprised when I got this part as I had never thought of myself as a Salvation Army-type of girl, but it was a good part and I really enjoyed playing it.

Gigs like that were to die for. They also meant that Mike and I got to spend lots more quality time together, which we both deeply appreciated. Mike's new company prospered and was quickly becoming the industry leader in Hong Kong. He used to tell me that his big ambition was to have a completely Chinese management team, and he achieved that. As the contracts of the ex-pat management team expired, he would replace them with well-trained Chinese managers.

One of his interests was quality assurance, and he would teach his young managers, but it was to backfire because his staff were always headhunted by other companies in the industry. However, I think he was secretly quite proud of that. His company became the first construction company in Hong Kong to be awarded the International Quality Assurance certificate, ISO 9001/9002, which was quite an honour, but in reality it was the result of some very hard work.

We celebrated this by taking a holiday on the beautiful island of Bali. I had decided that I wanted to change my lifestyle and I wanted to eat differently. So when we awoke the next morning we went down to breakfast and there, laid out before us, was the most amazing array of fruit you have ever seen – so exotic you could not believe it could exist.

A few days before we left I had bought a book called *Fit For Life,* and this, for me, turned out to be a life-changer. I am sure that by now most people have heard of this famous book. I told Mike that I would start to practise its ethic when we landed in Bali, and during our two-week holiday I had lost two and a half pounds, just as the book had forecast. That was a wonderful holiday in Bali back in 1980, and it is still one of my favourite memories.

When I was back in Hong Kong my friend Linda, who was by now my very best friend, planned my future. I used to go to the Health Club and talk to other members about it, and I remember Linda saying to me that she thought I was being just a little 'over the top'. That did not faze me because now, beside my show business career, I had another major interest - health.

Before joining the Phillip Wain Health Club I had been with other health clubs in Hong Kong where some of the instructors had not been qualified, because some of the exercises were not only difficult but very dangerous. So when I was able, I took a three-month sabbatical from show business and took a twelve-week course. It was quite an intense course which included both practical and theory work. At the end of the course came the exams, and I passed with quite good marks. I was then sent to another good health club on Hong Kong Island to gain experience as an instructor.

During my career I had kept in touch with the boss of Phillip Wain's health club, and she told me that if I qualified she would love to employ me. And so she did. Being a new instructor, my first class was at 7.30 am. We were expected to look the part, complete with make-up and contact lenses, and be wearing the correct clothes, which were supplied by the club - it was just like show business! At the time the young instructors were teaching classes in Hi-Lo Impact, Stretch, Step and many others, but they were not qualified and a lot of the movements were very difficult. Not only that, they were being taught wrongly, which could be quite dangerous.

So off I went and a took another three-month course with the University of Canada. When I finished, of course, I had to be tested to qualify. You had to sit a written theory exam and then put a one-hour class together with Warm-Up, Lo-Impact into Hi-Impact, Cooldown and Stretch, full body stretch and finish. All of this had to be set to music on a cassette tape which perfectly matched the workout routine. Let me tell you, you're never going to get that right first time, but I managed to do it, and qualified as an instructor.

Philip Wain gave me a job, but I had to look the part for it - make-up even at 7.30 am, contact lenses and clothing with logos to advertise the club. I worked for Philip for about five years, at all four clubs. It was an absolute pleasure. I was getting a bit older, but was still able to boast the body of a young girl!

So now my singing career was taking something of a back seat. I was very choosy with what I wanted to do. By now I had good contacts at the TV and radio stations and I would go out and do commercials, just as Gene and I had done many, many years before in Bermuda. Strangely, my singing became even more of a pleasure, probably because I was doing less. I was absolutely over the moon - a great husband and a full life. To say that I enjoyed Hong Kong would have been a major understatement. If you were a workaholic, as I was, Hong Kong definitely worked for you.

It went without saying that as a married couple we worked together the best we could. We lived by our diaries. It was no use having a full diary if Mike was not able to take a break, and it was no use him taking a break if I had a full diary, so I learned to communicate with his secretary, a lovely Hong Kong girl who spoke better English than Mike or me. It always seemed to work well.

We would come back to Portugal and always enjoyed our time together. On one trip we rented a nice little house in the town of Albufeira, in the Algarve. We had by now explored this part of the Algarve, and loved it, so we spent our hard-earned money and bought our first home together. Looking back, we still laugh and wonder if we did the right thing. Living and working so far away, it was quite impossible to look after the fabric of the house, and so the years when we took our holidays in Portugal consisted of maintaining our property, which was really hard work! On the other hand, we had established ourselves in Portugal and got to learn that the only negative aspect of the country was the all-pervading bureaucracy, which in our view held the country back, but that is another story.

Back in Hong Kong I had made many friends, and our favourite day was Sunday. There was a music bar in Kowloon known as Ned Kelly's, where the stage was as big as the rest of the bar and attracted all the top musicians in the colony. The place used to heave with people, even some from the UK Philharmonic

Orchestra, and it was totally multi-racial. It was a wonderful example of just how the world was designed, by God, to live. The money was poor, but it was the most wonderful evening you could wish for. Some of the clientele were real Old Colonial types, lovely people, with wrinkled sunburned skin, and in most cases, a distinct lack of teeth, but a great pleasure to talk with!

Mike became used to working seven days a week as well as Christmas and Easter holidays. Remember the Chinese people are Buddhist, and only recognised Christmas on a commercial level. So we did not see him every Sunday evening, but he knew I was well taken care of.

The Chinese and British Governments had started negotiating the takeover of Hong Kong within a couple of years, and it did not appear that things were going very well. The atmosphere in Hong Kong seemed to change, little by little, and no one was really sure what the outcome would be.

This was 1989, and a few months later came the Tiananmen Square massacre in Beijing, when hundreds of people were killed after protesting against the oppressive regime. It was very sad, and may I say, very frightening, even for us in Hong Kong. Mike took it all quite badly and I could see he was no longer as happy as I had known him. He never discussed the situation, but as a woman I can see these things. I often wonder if he felt this way because he worked for a Chinese Government company. So I was beginning to see the writing on the wall.

Mike's attitude was beginning to change. He had established a very successful company. He had to report to his Chinese bosses every month and they were happy with what he was achieving, but he used to talk about his supply chain, and say that a company such as his could only work well with its supply chain intact. I would nod my head wisely, but never had a clue, in reality, as to what he was talking about.

For him, things were changing. The Directors of China Resources were changing, which was a shame as he had a very good relationship with them. To this day he has never said in any detail what was happening, but I could see he was getting less happy - in fact, he was getting depressed. I remember one day asking him if he wanted to leave Hong Kong. He told me he had put eight years into the company, so it was not an easy thing to do.

I knew we had three choices. We could go back to Bermuda, but Mike would not be able to work there. We could go to the UK, but the weather was horrible, and for me, that would not work. Or, we could go to Portugal. Portugal by now was an EU member country, and as such we were able to become permanent residents.

The months went by and it was becoming more apparent that Mike was no longer happy, so I sat him down and we discussed the alternatives. I was so amazed and so very happy when he chose Bermuda. He said God had been at his side all his life, so why would he desert him now? The next day he gave his directors six months' notice.

So, our second life in Hong Kong was to come to an end, but I was not sad, just very grateful that God had been so kind as to give me two wonderful experiences in fantastic Hong Kong.

As the industry grew, Michael felt it was time to let go of the reins, and this decision coincided with Hong Kong being handed to China in 1997. We had found our home in Portugal, and were invited to go back for a special occasion, when China Resources would thank Michael officially for all he had done, and been, in the construction industry; after all, he had been responsible for setting up the first ready-mixed concrete company for China. And how they thanked him! As a memento, after the most elaborate occasion you can imagine, the company presented him with a beautifully, intricately-carved bonsai tree, each leaf in a precious stone, as an expression of the gratitude of the Chinese people for all he had done for them during the past twenty years. It was just overwhelming, and the bonsai still takes pride of place in our home - away from the curiosity of the cat, of course.

CHAPTER 8

Return to Bermuda, 1994/1995

Before we left Hong Kong we had many goodbyes to say. Mike was upset to be leaving his Chinese staff as he felt very close to them. He did tell me, years later, of his feelings at this time. He said he felt like a traitor - suppose things had gone wrong in Hong Kong, and China had sent in the army? He would be safe, but his staff would not be. I think to this day that he still feels that way.

We did return to Hong Kong two years later, by invitation of his company. We had planned to stay for two weeks, but we left after eight days. The place just did not feel the same.

So we arrived in Bermuda not knowing what fate had in store for me. I had sold my home on the South Shore a few years before, and we found a nice house on the North Shore which we both liked, and purchased it.

When Michael and I returned to Bermuda for the first time, I have to say I did find it small and insular, and maybe I felt the shows weren't quite so exciting compared with the big tours such as China and Spain. I suppose it is true to say that this was the basic reason why I felt I needed to live off the island - my own perceptions had, quite naturally, changed. My eyes had been opened to the bigger picture of the world stage, professionally and metaphorically; however, and maybe the best feeling anyone in my job could carry with them - I knew that in Bermuda I had learned everything that was worth learning, and Bermuda is where my roots remain - that can never change.

My immediate job was to find some work - after all, I had a husband to keep! But within only a few weeks of talking to entertainers and musicians it dawned on me that Bermuda had changed. It was no longer the same happy and contented country I had left in 1978 to join Bubbling Brown Sugar. Many entertainers and musicians were no longer working. At first, the causes of the problem did not sink in.

I did manage to negotiate nights at the Sonesta Beach, the Grotto Bay, the Elbow Beach and the Hamilton Princess, so we worked four nights a week.

The Hamilton Princess was the only hotel that had an opening act, then the main act - mainly American or English performers - so every night they had a different Bermudian act. Gene and I opened shows for the stars, such as Kenny Rogers, Sammy Davis Jr., Ella Fitzgerald, Sarah Vaughan and Bette Midler.

Bette was rather like Barbara Streisand but had a different character in her voice. Bette is such a performer, larger than life, with a voice which can almost 'say' a song.

I remember so well the singer Barry Manilow coming with Bette. He was very shy. At that time, of course, we did not know who he was, nor who he was to become. He was simply her arranger and piano accompanist, and conducted the band. Soon, however, he was to become the big star with his songs, including, of course, *Mandy*.

I was yet to meet the management of the Southampton Princess. I finally went to a meeting with the management there accompanied by the President of the Musicians' Union, and to this day I cannot remember why he was there. There was a strange atmosphere to the meeting of a kind I had never come across before. I felt that I was not wanted, yet they still wanted to talk. No matter how hard I tried, it seemed impossible to get any answers from the management. In the end, I said goodbye, saying that maybe we could speak again.

Within days, the evening I had been promised was

filled by the President of the Union and his band. The Southampton Princess had a show running in the showroom made up of all Americans, and not one Bermudian. And as I looked around the Island I could see many white British entertainers working - taking jobs from Bermudians. I spoke to the President of the Union, asking what was happening. I never got a satisfactory answer. I went to the Immigration Department and asked how these people were working at the Southampton Princess. I never got a satisfactory answer there either.

All this was a shock. I remember the tourist industry as having been built on love and great service, with this love being reciprocated by the tourists to the staff. This in my opinion was the foundation of the tourist industry, backed up by wonderful entertainers and musicians. I think of Gene Steede, in my opinion Bermuda's top entertainer ever, the Talbot Brothers, the Strollers, the Esso Steede Band, Bootsie and many, many more wonderful talents, and you know what they say: 'If you don't use it, you lose it'. And in this industry, that is a fact.

I sometimes thumb through *Jazz of the Rock* and *Musicians on the Rock,* two wonderful entertainment histories by Dale Butler MP. Many of the people mentioned in those books have passed away, and others have left the industry. The loss is Bermuda's. I forecast with confidence that it will be well-nigh impossible for Mr Butler to add a third book.

Bermuda years ago was very good to me, and for that I will always be grateful. I continued to talk to the President of the Musicians' Union, who one day even threatened me with expulsion from the Union. I asked the Immigration Department one simple question: 'How were work permits issued to the foreign entertainers without the job seeming to be advertised?' I never got a satisfactory answer. I wrote many letters to the *Royal Gazette*, trying to stir the pot. What was more unbelievable was that I got no backup from my own entertainment industry. This was a one-sided war of attrition which continued for many months, and there was only going to be one loser - me.

Mike gave me my head. He never interfered, except for sometimes helping me to wipe my tears. It was a terrible time for me. I had no one helping me in my corner, although I was 100% sure that this crusade was worth it.

Suddenly, I lost the Hamilton Princess. I don't know why, as the evenings were well-supported, but I was not surprised. This was followed by the Elbow Beach a few weeks later. They suddenly replaced me and others with an old guy from England and a state-of-the-art, very expensive, organ. You see, I was being starved into submission.

I have tried to explain in simple terms my few months as a woman, trying to take on some very powerful interests. I came a very poor second. To this day I have no idea why, but this state of affairs was asking to be questioned, and to this day I still do just that.

I still talk with Gene - after all, we have two children together. I find it incredible that a God-given talent such as his has been reduced to taking scraps thrown by the hotels. It was clear that my best efforts would not change anything. No one was listening!

It was clear there would be no future for me in Bermuda, so we sold our house and made plans to move to Portugal.

I have just two thoughts on this unhappy state of affairs. Firstly, in my opinion the hotel and restaurant industry made a serious error when they agreed to the 'service charge'. To this day I have not met one serious person who agrees that it's a good idea. I was not in Bermuda at the time, but I have been told that the whole atmosphere surrounding service changed uncomfortably quickly. Many employees in the industry no longer had to earn their tips. It surely was a recipe for disaster. I have learned through many years in this industry that atmosphere is so very important. I am aware that I have oversimplified the tourism problem, but every journey has a start and a finish. I know this, because I have made a few journeys.

Secondly, I will say this. Entertainment is a very important part of the tourism industry, and you mess it up at your peril. Electronic entertainment will never work long term. Visitors can get that anywhere in the world. What they want, although they may not realise it, is the warmth and love provided by live entertainment. They will realise it if they are being provided with anything less. It amazes me that hotel managers have never realised that your very best and cheapest form of advertisement is a visitor going home telling everyone who will listen what a wonderful Bermuda they visited, and what helped make it so wonderful was the entertainers.

CHAPTER 9

Discovering Portugal, 1995

Deciding to live in Portugal permanently was perhaps the best decision we ever made - from a financial standpoint to peace of mind and to the people. The Portuguese are probably the most generous of spirit and most likeable people I have ever lived amongst, and we have lived with many different peoples. Here we have the wonderful weather, the ability to support ourselves, and as long as we can do it legally, we can live here in Portugal. So we have a wonderful people to live with, a way to support ourselves, a way to make a little money, and the most amazing weather anywhere in the world. As we are living in Europe we can work as long as we want to. You may not make the kind of money you would make when you were younger, but then you are not younger. I guess what I mean is that it is just peaceful!

We decided that we loved it, and more importantly, because it reminded us of Bermuda, this this was where we would like to live. We have now been living and working in the Algarve, and loving it, for nineteen years.

When we first came here, on 1st April 1995, it really was like stepping back in time. It is stunningly beautiful and the people are lovely. We have never lived in any of the cities, always preferring the quieter side of life - Michael coming from Portsmouth on the south coast of England, while I of course was from Bermuda. The area in which we live is very similar to where I spent my formative years. The Algarve, with its terracotta-tiled rooftops, bright sunshine and lovely people, so reminds me of Bermuda and its people. All you have to imagine is the white rooftops and you can easily imagine Bermuda. And then people talk to you, actually speak to you in the mornings or whenever they pass you on the street, something that is also very Bermudian. The children are, in every circumstance, very, very respectful.

Because you simply cannot go into any country without being able, financially and otherwise, to care for yourself and other things, and because we already owned a home here, all our residency procedures went fairly well and quite quickly, including ID cards, drivers' licences, medical cards and social security cards. Now we could get down to business!

Mike had already bought into a scuba diving business, where he was partnered with a local resident who had lived here for many years. Now all I had to do was find work, which I had never had a problem with! I worked all over the Algarve, starting with Albufeira town centre. I did it all, I covered it all. All the restaurants, all the hotels – I've done them. So there was nothing left for me to do but break into the casinos, which I have also done, but on a rather smaller scale.

We have owned property here in Portugal for over thirty years, and of course we have tried, diligently, to learn to speak Portuguese. We have accomplished this quite well, but we do realise that we will have to continue conversational classes forever as we get older. There is sometimes a problem when you start off learning proper (Lisbon) Portuguese, and then live on the south coast where they speak colloquial Portuguese - you might have a little problem with people laughing at you!

We live in the village of Paderne near the town of Albufeira. Every morning I walk through the village and up again into the hills, and I meet everybody. In the winter, of course, the time is different; I go at 7.30 am, and in the summer at 6 am, and as you can imagine, the people vary, but let's just say I know all the tractor drivers and bus drivers, all the school kids and working people, and after almost twenty years it's all change, but amazingly so. All the kids that we first saw going to school have grown up, and the working people have aged, while the older people - lots of them - have passed on. But then, that's what happens when you are living in a country, rather than visiting it.

When we first arrived on April 1st 1995 after selling our home on the North Shore side of Bermuda, as I said, we already owned a home here so all we had to do was move in. It was a gated community in Albufeira called 'Alto do Moinho' - so, so lovely, overlooking the beach and ocean, but because we had not been living here but merely visiting we had no idea of how Albufeira had grown. So, by the time we had opened our packing crates we pretty much knew that we would be moving again, and since then we have never been close to living near a city, even a small one. Again, of course, we then went through all the bureaucracy of living here, setting up home here, banks, accountants, all my own music. All my own gowns, and of course, the capability to meet anywhere in the country. So we said, or thought, why not? My dancer and producer friend Simon Duvall very cleverly figured that with all the gowns of many different colours that I had, and all the costumes he could make, he could turn this combination into a very interesting stage show - and he did! And so we became a troupe. We travelled far and wide in Europe.

When we arrived in Portugal and moved into our house, we had a container bring our belongings over from Bermuda. This was in 1995. During our months in Bermuda we had boxes which we had never unpacked from Hong Kong. I was confident that in one of these were my diaries, newspaper clippings and photographs. I never opened that box in Bermuda as I had no need of them.

It was not until we arrived in Portugal and we were unpacking everything that I suddenly realised my treasured box of souvenirs was missing. To this day I have no idea how or when it was lost, but it has made writing this story of my life very difficult. It means I must rely on my memory plus the memories of other dear friends and family, so I apologise if time lines are sometimes a little hazy. I may have missed some important days of my life, and for that I apologise also.

I have already mentioned Portuguese bureaucracy. It was a nightmare for two people who were unable to speak the language. The thing I remember best was the queues. But we had to stick with it, because a whole lot of paperwork was required to settle in this beautiful country. I had not yet started thinking of working in Portugal as we were still organising our future life, and I was still feeling bruised in mind and spirit from my unpleasant experience in Bermuda.

This did not stop me from doing my five-mile walk early every morning. Walking in an area called Montechoro one Sunday morning - it must have been around 7.30 - I spotted people coming out of a place called Café La Rose. They were not yobs, but quite well-dressed and very attractive men and women. I had a look at the photos outside, and what I saw was a small theatre, laid out with tables and chairs and a small stage. This intrigued me, and I was determined to find out more.

A few days later I went again to the Café La Rose, this time in the afternoon. I knocked on the main door and a gentleman came out. I asked if he spoke English and when he answered yes, I introduced myself. He in return told me his name was Carlos, but that his stage name was Guido Scarletti. I was to find out that he was a very famous entertainer in Portugal. He told me he owned the Café La Rose. I had already fallen in love with the place. I had a backing track in my bag - it was 'Don't Cry for Me, Argentina'. He turned on his marvellous sound system and I sang, just for him.

He gave me a job immediately. He explained that the Club did not open until midnight, his clientele being mostly hotel management and staff and show people. Now, I ask you, was God looking after me, or what?

He asked if I could do my show at 1.30 in the morning. The money was not great but he would send a car to my house to pick me up at 12.30 and a car would bring me home after the show. I really thought I had died and gone straight to heaven. Carlos wrote a musical for his stage, which was called 'Evita Forever'.

It was quite beautiful, and of course, I sang 'Argentina'. I was a lucky girl.

However, all good things come to an end, and the late nights were taking their toll, so I spoke with Carlos and left Café La Rose. It is now closed, and that, surely, must be Portugal's loss. However, from that one job at the Café La Rose I was able to get other work in Albufeira, hotels and restaurants. It was not what I wanted to do, but it was all I could get.

Mike and I loved exploring Portugal, especially the hilly regions. That was how we found the little village where we now live, Paderne. When we first stumbled across it we had a great meal in what was at that time the village's only restaurant. We explored an old castle built by the Arabs when they ran the show in Portugal, and decided that this was where we would actually like to settle. So we quickly sold our house and acquired a nice one on the outskirts of Paderne, called Almeijoafras - try saying that with a couple of glasses of wine already in you!

By now we were learning Portuguese, and I am proud to say I was doing better than Mike. He was finding the language hard work. I met a lady from South Africa who had spent most of her life in Angola, which was at one time a Portuguese colony. Her Portuguese is perfect and she and I have been friends for many years now, and we always have conversations in Portuguese. I do have a problem, however, in that I get a little nervous when I talk to anyone else, but never mind, I am told my grammar is good. I still lack vocabulary, but it is coming, slowly.

The casinos in the Algarve were now off-limits for me. They were putting on wonderful stage shows, mostly with fantastic Russian dancers. The producer of one of these shows offered me a starring role in a major production she was putting on in the Casino Espinho, which is near Oporto. It was a minimum six-month contract, a great production, and I was now in my life a more mature performer surrounded by much younger Portuguese and English kids. It reminded me, in many ways, of Bubbling Brown Sugar - shows every night and rehearsals every day. But I still loved it! I was supplied with a nice apartment and Mike would come up every weekend.

After my six months was up I called it a day and went back down to Albufeira. During the show at Espinho I had met an English guy, a dancer and producer called Simon Duvall, who I mentioned earlier. Simon used to mount shows for many of the big nightclubs in Spain and Portugal. He was a really wonderful guy. We talked and talked, and began to realise that we could work together. So we joined forces and did many of the major clubs and casinos up north. He always told me he was in negotiations with the Tourism Authority of the Chinese Government. Because he knew I had spent many years in Hong Kong, I always thought he was pulling my leg. But then one day I had a call from him saying the China tour was on. I was both amazed and ecstatic.

So I met Simon and the rest of the cast at Madrid airport before flying to Beijing - this was late 1995. It was a cultural visit, showing the Chinese people how the rest of the world looked. We had three days for rehearsals, but Simon had chosen a skilled cast, and after three days we were ready, mainly because we had all worked with him before.

The theatres were absolutely amazing. I was told that the majority of them held at least 3,000 people. The audience did not pay, as I was told they were bussed in from surrounding areas and the shows were part of their education. Amazing!

We did Beijing, Shanghai and many of the other marvellous cities, which were just a blur. In Hong Kong I had learned some Cantonese, which was the Chinese language spoken there, so I had promised that I would do the announcing in the show, not realising that the Northern Chinese did not speak Cantonese but Mandarin. So I had to learn some announcements in Mandarin, by rote. It was embarrassing, but nobody seemed to mind. The audiences were ecstatic.

I would open the show with a couple of songs, then introduced a few acts, then do a middle spot, then close the show with a big closing number along with all the dancers. Then I would bow off and introducing all the speciality acts. Quite spectacular – and we were accompanied by an interpreter who could step in to help us at all times. I never got to work in Australia or Moscow – maybe in the next life...

The theatres were bigger and better than anything on Broadway or the West End. We were put up at the best hotels in whichever town we were in, and as I said - and it cannot be repeated enough - the venues were superb, and they were not only in the best hotels, but with meals three times a day and all the fine Chinese food you could eat. If we had (and it wasn't often) a blank night, they laid on something for us to do, such as seeing the Great Wall.

However, it was slowly dawning on me that I was no longer a young woman. I had a conversation one day with a Chinese guide, and told her that I could not believe the audience liked me so much. She put a bomb under me by telling me that I was respected because I was older. Oh dear! Admittedly I was now in my sixties. But the Chinese venerate age, and they treated me as someone truly special. They were always perfectly courteous when they ventured backstage and queued to seek my autograph, as I was regarded as someone of wisdom and experience, as well as an entertainer. 'Do you enjoy this work? Do you ever get tired?' they would ask, in that sincere, deferential manner which the real Chinese have. My response was always sincere too, as I was truly touched by their adulation and wanted to show them my own gratitude. Simon was a little less responsive, even if they did speak perfect English, but each to his own. I felt truly enriched by their reaction to me and could feel the bond of warmth between myself and these lovely people.

On our days off our guides took us to the Great Wall of China and Tiananmen Square, the Palace of the People. It was all incredible. Mike and I really appreciated the Chinese people. We admired their work ethic, their artistic ability and above all, their niceness and their kindness. We were so grateful to spend so much time with them.

When I came to Portugal, I met the British actor Clive Dunn, famous for his song 'Granddad' and later for being one of the stars of the BBC sitcom 'Dad's Army'. Clive had moved to Portugal in the 1980s and had settled there, enjoying his hobby of painting. I had come from the West End of London and was booked to go to the Olive Press in Tavira, where they do jazz nights. Clive came and made himself known to me. Although I was not familiar with his hit song I had seen him in 'Dad's Army', and we became warm friends.

On November 2 2012 I performed with Clive in the Lagoa Community Centre. Clive opened the first part of the show, but he told our promoter, Jenny Grainer, to 'Let Pinky close the show because she's younger than me'! The show went down so well that we were invited back to do it again the following year, but sadly Clive passed away just four days later on November 6, aged 92. However, I had already told Jenny her that I would do the show again, and sure enough I did. It was my privilege to pay tribute to Clive when the show opened again on 2nd November 2013.

By now I was beginning to enjoy our life in Portugal, as we had made many friends. I was realising that my childhood ambitions to be a superstar would never be. I had my marriage, my neighbours, my dog, my cat Tilly, and I am still in contact with my kids and family in Bermuda via Skype. I had slowly reduced my workload. I gave all my sound equipment, gowns and music to the Paderne Town Band and I am told they still use a lot of the stuff. I made a CD called 'Colours' which was well-received, and I can look back on a career which was fairly successful. Now I do whatever charity work I can, and I am pleased just to be able to put my love and affection back into society. God has been kind to me in my life.

Just one last thought: In 2009 I was included in the Bermuda Music Hall of Fame - a proud day for me.

CHAPTER 10

A hurricane and a charity show, 2004

I have just returned from Bermuda in my more professional persona, Miss Pinky Steede, having been invited to perform for PALS cancer care on my island. PALS has been operating for many years on the island, helping, many, many people, some of whom have been in my own family. The country has had them for almost 35 years - a very lucky country and a very lucky people.

When I first arrived on the island I was, as always, struck first by the sheer beauty of the place, and then by the generosity of the people. Everyone is so open - "Good Morning", "How are you doing this morning?"

"Have a nice day!" It's so lovely that you almost don't mind spending your money.

I was to do two shows, one being the PALS Gala Evening, where all the very big and important companies on the Island vie for a place at the very expensive tables; they are sold to raise money for PALS because obviously it takes quite a lot of money to run an organisation such as this.

Would you believe, the very first weekend we were hit by a tropical storm. We actually all went to bed afterwards, and much to our surprise we had to get up again, having been hit by something more. The island was flattened and for some strange reason we had slept through it. When we awoke and finally left the house, we discovered that there were many houses in quite close proximity to ours that we had not seen because the trees (which were now flattened) were hiding them.

We thought: "Okay, fine!" We walked from Ferry Reach into the Square of St George, only to discover that everything was off - electricity, water, everything. But right up front, I've got to tell you, we had the best time. I've always thought we probably take too many showers anyway! It was the best holiday we had had in a very long time.

But now, don't get too comfortable because, remember, I had come to my home country to do a job of work - performing!

But getting back to the storm, it was absolutely

diabolical. I could not believe that we had slept all the way through it, and when we walked out the devastation was absolutely astounding. It was as though God had decided the Island needed a good cleaning up, so he had set about doing it. And it was Island-wide; every roof that could be blown off, was; every tree that could be flattened, was; electric wires down, slates blown off rooftops, fences smashed. Boats had been lifted out of the water, and in some instances set down on the land.

Having walked into St George, we found its centre very still. The most wonderful thing of all was the discovery that no one had been injured or killed.

The powers that be on Bermuda very quickly set about putting the Island back together and making it operational again. The islanders were on their feet immediately following the storm, kind of "all hands on deck" - an amazing thing to see! But something I remember quite well.

I continued my rehearsals and my daily walks into St George - but wait, would you believe it, the following Friday there came another hurricane. This time it was male (they take it in turns). The first one was called Faye, and this guy was called Gonzalo, the strongest hurricane to hit the Atlantic for four years. He was the same fella who went on to kill three people in Ireland.

I'm getting ahead of myself though, because, Faye also created havoc - everywhere really, on the island. But when Gonzalo blew in just the next weekend -

OMG, you have never seen anything like it. Well, I haven't at any rate. This guy was the proverbial bully, because he struck, it seemed, quite early in the evening and no one, and I do mean no one (except my Michael), could sleep. Gonzalo, tried to bully his way into our house and was not amused when we did not, repeat did not, get up out of bed and let him in. He was vicious, and it was possibly the most frightening experience of my life. I say that quite categorically. He wanted the roof off, he wanted the windows and doors out, and most of all he wanted us.

Fortunately our niece and nephew, with whom we were staying on the island at

Ferry Reach, with Michael, had diligently put up boardings with a friend, and Gonzalo could not break them. Amen!

The eye of the hurricane passed over the Island roughly between three o'clock and five,
and I swear to God that this storm covered all the 23 miles length and three miles width of Bermuda. The eye of a storm - now this I had never experienced before - is like no other experience I've had. You know when a large cat has a small mouse between its paws and is just doing the old cat-and-mouse game, batting it from one paw to the other? Gonzalo was doing much the same as that with us. There was not a sound. You know old folks always tell you you could hear a pin drop? When that happens it scares the bejasus out of people. I wish I was clever enough to make you, the

reader, feel this experience. There is nothing to compare to it - it was like someone, or something, had their hand clasped over your mouth and nose, and was double-daring you to struggle.

It seemed that just as quickly as it came, it was gone, but it was not over that quickly.

In the St George Foundation, Executive Director Charlotte Andrews said the charity which looked after the *Deliverance* (the ship in St George) would have to conduct a detailed assessment of the vessel. The story of the *Deliverance* is linked closely with hurricanes. It was built by the survivors of the 1609 wreck of the *Sea Venture*, itself driven onto the reefs of Bermuda's eastern end after being separated from its fleet by a hurricane. This was the incident that is said to have inspired William Shakespeare in what many believe was his last play, *The Tempest*, and of course Gonzalo is one of the characters in it.

The dockyard which my brother Howard (Tilly) Caisey had helped to build all those many years ago sustained much damage. All of the large ships which go into Bermuda full of tourists dock in the Dockyard now, because Hamilton and St George Dock are just too small to accommodate them any more. When we left Bermuda almost the entire house had electricity, water and everything necessary to run the island.

I must tell you about two incidents which we observed after Hurricane Gonzalo. Firstly, the coming together of the island's peoples, black and white and indifferent- an amazing thing to see - and secondly, the ships which came into the island to offer help; the small planes which flew in from (I'm guessing) the east coast of the US - all of this to see if any help was necessary. It just made me realize, once again, how very blessed this little island of mine and its 68,000 or so inhabitants really are. I think perhaps all of this was greatly helped by the authorities on the island, from the Premier down to and including the Regiment of the Royal Navy.

And now - the "Show". Finally I got the call from my sponsors on the island, Patricia and Sidney Purvey, that the show was on:

'PALS' (Cancer Care in Bermuda) presents a
Matinee Concert

with

PINKY STEEDE

at the Fairmont Southampton Princess Hotel

October 26 2014

Yeeeha! And so off we went to present ourselves at the hotel for our tech rehearsal at 11 o'clock Sunday morning. Because at home I have my own studio, I do all my preparation before I get to wherever l happen to be performing. All my music is professionally arranged and recorded by a friend of mine, arranger

Duncan Kinell, and any extra voicings which are heard on the CDs are done by Duncan and his wife, "France" Duncan. I have worked with them for many years, and it has been my extreme pleasure.

The rehearsal and sound were conducted by my long-time friend Barry Fitzsimmons and his brother Julian. Josh Whisky ran the machine with my CDs and I think he discovered why each song had to be recorded separately - I am a great talker. Whisky is the son of another very well-known, wonderful singer on the island, Mr Calvin Hendrickson, and is very musical. By the time I had finished the hour or so of rehearsing, I knew my voice was in exactly the right place.

The show went very, very well. I earned a standing ovation, and I was very happy with that. But as if that was not enough, I was joined on stage by my ex-singing partner and ex-husband, the father of my son and daughter Jay and Crystal - Gene Steede. I went absolutely wild. Of course we knew nothing of this because performers are turned deaf and blind by the sound and lights, but because we had not sung together on a professional stage for some years - we think 35 or 40 - the audience of Bermudians loved it, and so did we!

Oh yes, and after my show it was suggested I might like to consider performing at the Bermuda Festivals, which happen around January, February and March, and of course I said "Yes please!"

POSTSCRIPT: As this book was going to press, I received a phone call from Bermuda to tell me that the Bermuda Arts Council has awarded me a Lifetime Achievement Award. What a wonderful way to end my book!

www.ingramcontent.com/pod-product-compliance
Lightning Source LLC
Chambersburg PA
CBHW071700040426
42446CB00011B/1847